S0-AEU-363

Soul Contracts

How they affect your life and your relationships

by

Linda Baker

Patch work Press

For Robin,
May this book serve you well and may your life be filled with many. Blessings, Linda

Copyright © 1998 by Linda Baker

Published by Patchwork Press
An imprint of Tenacity Press
1-800-738-6721

All rights reserved. This book may not be reproduced in whole or in part, without written permission from the publisher, except by a reviewer who may quote brief passages in review, nor may any part of this book be reproduced, stored in a retrieval system, or transmitted in any form or by any means electronic, mechanical, photocopying, recording or other without written permission from the publisher.

Readers are cautioned that his book is not intended to replace advice or treatment for any medical or emotional problems. In the event that you use any of the information in this book for yourself, the author and publisher assume no responsibility for your actions.

ISBN 1-892193-01-9
Library of Congress Catalog card Number: 98-67602

Cover photo of Mount Rainier by Michael Baker
Taken Christmas Day 1997
with a Nikon camera, using a 210 mm lens.
Mount Rainier is approximately 14,000 feet and is located about seventy miles SE of Seattle, Washington

Printed by Morris Publishing
Cover design by Morris Publishing
3212 E Highway 30
Kearney NE 68847
1-800-650-7888

Second Edition 1999
10 9 8 7 6 5 4 3 2 1

Dedicated to everyone on a journey of love and forgiveness, and especially to Kate and her brother John for their tremendous courage.

The first peace,
which is most important,
is that which comes
within the souls of people
when they realize their relationship,
their oneness with the universe
and all its powers.

- Black Elk

Acknowledgments

I would first like to express my deepest gratitude to Spirit for guiding me on my life's journey. I am also grateful to Tom, my husband and best friend of twenty-eight years, for his love and endless support in the writing of this book and in all that I have endeavored to do in my life.

I thank our own children Vicki and Caleb, our adopted son Raymond, as well as our foster children for all the love and wisdom that I have gained through them. I am grateful to all of many wonderful friends, students, and clients whose stories and belief in me have inspired the writing of this book.

I wish to acknowledge the many friends who have shared their enthusiasm and faith in the production of *Soul Contracts* by purchasing a first edition book, sight unseen.

Soul Contracts may never have come to be without the professional and personal guidance and support from my writing teacher, Hal Zina Bennett and the publication support of Susan J. Sparrow. My thanks also to Danielle Williams for her invaluable editorial work, and to the Morris Publishing Company for their work in the final production of this book.

The stories in this book are drawn from real situations. Some of them are a composite of several similar stories. All of the names and identifying characteristics have been changed in keeping with client confidentiality. This differs only where I have have received permission, and on occasion, been requested to use the subject's true name. Because many of us share similar issues I have attempted to pick stories that others may find helpful.

The information in this book is meant to compliment the advice and guidance of your physician, not replace it, If you are under the care of a physician, you should discuss any major changes in your regimen with him or her. Because this is a book and not a medical consultation, keep in mind that the information presented here may not apply in you particular case. Whenever a question arises, discuss it with your physician.

Patronage is an old, time honored and important tradition in publishing. I have found that it is far more than financial support. The kind, encouraging words of each patron has inspired me to believe in myself and has motivated me to do my very best. Without you, this book would not be. I wish to acknowledge and thank each patron.

List of Patrons

Allen A. Allen
Carol Bach
Caleb Baker
Tom Baker
Donna Bardwell
Monty Berke & Anita Graham
Patty Berke & Georgia Sabol
Kathleen Boehm
Margaret Bowers
Anita Brennan
Mary Cain & David Slagle
Tom Des Brisay
Vicki & Bryan Fairbanks
Ric Giardina of *Spirit Employed*
Gigi & Peggy
George-Marie Glover
Eva Goldman
Sharyn Hadler
James & Rosemary Hughes
Cris Kantor
Deborah Kaye & Jan Van Ysslestyne
Judy Lochrie
Barry MacGray
Maria Michael & Anton A. Schwarzinger
Marie Morton
The *New Times* of Seattle
Bert & Jennifer Noia
Lori Olson & Kristine Lundein
Rod Rowan
Alice Spencer
Carol Wadsworth
Judy & David Ward
Marjaana Ylitalo

I no longer try to change the outer things. They are simply a reflection. I change my inner perception and the outer reveals the beauty so long obscured by my own attitude. I concentrate on my inner vision and find my outer view transformed. I find myself attuned to the grandeur of life and in unison with the perfect order of the universe.

- Daily Word

Table of Contents

Section IV - Personal Soul Contracts

Section V - A Spiritual Approach to Abortion

Section VI - In Conclusion

A word from the author

It appears that as the consciousness of our planet continues to grow and expand, the type of inner work needed for clearing and moving forward in life has shifted from where it was even a few years ago.

When I began my healing journey over thirty years ago, I found little to guide me and felt quite alone. Then came the early seventies and submerging oneself into the pain of the past and "being with the feelings" was what seemed to be required for healing. Therapies that encouraged screaming, pounding and reexperiencing one's pain became popular. At that time, I completely believed that, in order to heal, one had to experience nearly as much pain in therapy as was suffered during the original traumatic experience. To not go into the pain was to be in denial or avoidance and the promised relief of healing the trauma would be denied. For some reason, back then, this made sense to me.

From my personal experience and from the way my work with others has evolved, I no longer believe that reexperiencing one's pain is a necessity for healing. I have spoken with several people who are aware that they could use healing in their lives, but are unwilling to go back and reexperience the pain of their childhood. Actually they are not unwilling to feel feelings, but some have tried the screaming and pounding techniques and are just not interested in doing that over again. Others are not interested in "falling apart," as one person put it, and spending years in therapy. They have lives to live and want to live them. I feel there is wisdom in this. While therapy can help you to feel your feelings and to gain understanding, therapy doesn't need to become your life.

A long and diverse road brings me to my present place of experience and belief. In the pages that follow, my hope is to share experiences from my personal life as well as from the lives of clients and friends. Through these stories I hold the intention that you can find benefit, understanding and healing in your own life.

Section 1
Introduction

*It takes courage to grow up and turn out
to be who you really are.*

e.e. cummings

My Beginning

Great things are not done by impulse but by a series of small things brought together.
Vincent Van Gogh

From a very young age I was interested in why people did what they did. At twelve, I remember thinking a lot about the ways that my parents treated me. I started making a list of the things I wanted to remember not to do with my children when I grew up. I wondered why it was that I felt different from my family, and why many things that were important to them were not important to me, and vice versa. These questions led me to become an avid reader of psychology. The study of the mind and emotions was fascinating to me. At seventeen I left home and became a student of nursing.

During my first year at school, I decided to become a psychiatric nurse. I graduated, married and moved to Seattle where I took the state nursing examination and received my license as a Registered Nurse. My marriage lasted for one year. I didn't realize it at the time, but it was only the vehicle to bring me to Seattle where I could meet Tom, who is my life's partner.

When my husband, Tom, and I had our first child we decided that I would be a stay-at-home mom. I continued to volunteer for a mental health clinic, and since working with teenagers had become important to me, Tom and I began to foster parent emotionally challenged teens. With one of our first foster children, I was given the challenge of reparenting, something I knew nothing about. Six months after coming to live with us, the girl, whom I will call Beth, spontaneously regressed from her sixteen-year- old personality to that of about age four or five.

Beth had been experimenting with various drugs, had low self esteem, had dropped out of high school and was suicidal. Now she had let herself slip back into the emotional state of early childhood and needed love, support, and a structure that could help her to relearn some basic life beliefs such as, "I am loveable for who I am," "I am capable," and "My body is good." I wasn't sure what to do to help Beth, but I did remember back to a workshop that I attended several years earlier on reparenting schizophrenics. The woman who taught the workshop had written a book that I now went right out and bought, then stayed up all night reading. Although Beth was not schizophrenic, this book did give me confidence and direction in caring for her.

After six intense months of regressive work, Beth "grew up" and became a teenager again, but this time with a healthier attitude about herself and her life. From this experience I saw how it was possible for unhealthy, learned core beliefs to be replaced with new, more healthy and supportive ones. I had always believed that the only way to really heal was to go to the core of the issue. The gift of my relationship with Beth showed me how true this was. Just as a cut which has a grain of sand imbedded within it needs the irritant removed to prevent infection and heal, so the psyche needs release from negative thoughts and beliefs to be free and whole.

As I continued searching to find ways that would help myself and others to heal unhealthy core beliefs, I was introduced to Alchemical Hypnotherapy. This was back in 1985 when I only associated hypnotherapy with someone taking control of my mind by dangling a watch in front of my face, saying, "You are getting sleepy" or doing something weird that would make me cluck like a chicken. Indeed, I wouldn't have been interested in exploring hypnotherapy at all except that I was given a book by David Quigley entitled *Alchemical Hypnotherapy*. As I read through the pages of this book, I caught a glimpse of how reparenting work could be accomplished in a much shorter time by assisting the client in finding their own inner resources. This was a very exciting concept to me and prompted me to begin studying this healing art.

I began this journey by taking a four-day Hypnotherapy workshop on Alchemical Hypnotherapy with David Quigley. On the morning of the second day of the workshop, I awoke experiencing a difficulty in breathing and feeling as if I were being strangled to death. I knew that I needed to find the source of this feeling, quickly! I prayed to know what my body was trying to tell me. The message came through very clearly: "Leave the hospital. If you stay, it will kill you emotionally and spiritually. You need to follow another path." At that moment I knew that I had only one choice, and that was to listen to spirit and deepen my knowledge of this work. I am thankful that I made this choice because Alchemical Hypnotherapy has deeply affected my life as well as the lives of my clients.

At this time I was working as a psychiatric nurse in the adolescent unit of a small, private hospital. When

I returned to work, the day after David's workshop, I was again given the message to leave. As I opened the front doors of the hospital, I felt a gray air of depression envelop me. It was depression coming from the staff, not the patients. As I spoke with my co-workers I found that many of them were unhappy and feeling unfulfilled by their work. I also noticed a new patient, a young man of eighteen.

Within moments of my coming onto the unit the young man sat down next to me and began talking about how he was certain that something had happened to him when he was a small child. He couldn't recall what it was, but he expressed an interest in hypnotherapy as a way of finding out. This was both a surprise and a confirmation of the previous day's message. No other patient in all of my years at the hospital had ever mentioned hypnotherapy to me. I left my job a few weeks later so that young man could come to live with us. We did work together using the Alchemical Hypnotherapy techniques that I had learned and he did uncover and heal early childhood abuse issues which had robbed him of his power.

When I began practicing hypnotherapy more than a decade ago, I was still attached to the *pain + suffering = healing* equation. I always made certain that clients would stay in their pain long enough for me to feel that they were not avoiding or denying anything. The key words here are: "for me to feel." I now see that the therapist must be completely free of judgement, limitation, or expectation if the client is going to be able to heal in the fastest and most optimum way.

It was fortunate, that despite my own beliefs, the work proved to be very powerful and my clients experienced amazing results. Rather than dealing with symptoms, I found that the core of any issue was not only reachable, but healable. I saw more profound results with this system than with any of the traditional and alternative therapies that I had previously studied and used because clients by-passed the symptoms and went directly to the core of their issues.

I was excited about the potential of this work, continued training with David Quigley, and became certified as an Alchemical Hypnotherapist.

I could never have imagined the path that has unfolded before me. I believe that when we are open to new possibilities our consciousness expands, and if we do not become attached to what we do, our work continues to evolve. This is exactly what happened for me. I began to feel energy pouring out of my hands as I gave hypnotherapy sessions. Though I wasn't sure what to do with this energy, I vaguely remembered reading something about "smoothing auras." An inner voice told me to take Reiki. This was baffling to me. I didn't know what Reiki was, or even how to pronounce the word. However, after a period of several months I was led to a healing circle where Reiki was used, and eventually found my teachers and studied this energy system. I have learned to trust my inner voice. This voice has led me on an incredible journey, with every step touched by magic and love.

Soul Contracts

A New Practice Is Born

As I began combining energy work with hypno-therapy, my consciousness continued to open and expand, and I was awakened to new possibilities. After about two years of using these systems in combination, a client who had been terribly abused throughout her childhood and into adolescence came to me. This client had gone through many years of therapy, much of it centered around anger release work. At the beginning of our session together I encouraged her to move into these angry feelings so that she could express them in the way that I had been taught. She refused. She said that she had yelled, screamed, and punched enough pillows. She was tired of the anger and wanted to do something that would release her from it's grip. She wouldn't follow the rules I had been taught and I felt at a loss about what I could do.

As she lie before me, waiting, I remembered that the work I do is guided by spirit and it is not me, but Spirit (God), who assists the client in embracing healing. I turned the session over to Spirit. By this I mean, I got out of the way. I let go of my ego's need to find the answer and I acknowledged that a higher power than myself held the answer for this woman. I said a silent prayer asking that I be a clear vessel and that God work through me for her highest good.

I was guided to ask my client if she could notice in some way where the anger was located in her body. She responded that it was everywhere. "What color is it?" I asked. "Black," she said. "It's gooey and black and it's everywhere." I then asked her what she needed to do with this gooey, black anger, and she told me that she needed to let it drain out of her body. "How can you drain this from your body?" I asked. She felt and imagined a drain, like a bathtub drain, in the soles of both of her feet. I suggested that she begin to allow this black, gooey stuff to release from each and every cell and move out through these drains at the bottom of her feet.

As she began the process she became more relaxed and peaceful. She imagined this substance going down deep into the core of the earth where it became purified. With my hands held about six inches above her body, I began to do energy work. By this I mean that I imagined the energy from Spirit moving through my hands and assisting her to do the work. I moved my hands gently over her body in a downward motion from her head to her toes. After about ten minutes she said that the process was complete. There was none of the old energy left. I asked that she check each cell with her mind's eye and make certain that it was all clean and clear. After this I asked what she would like to fill this space with. She chose a bright, gold light and together we worked to bring this light into every cell of her body.

After our session, this woman told me that she felt more relaxed, calm and peaceful than she could ever remember having felt before. The important thing here is that she was able to anchor these peaceful, calm feelings into her life and continue to bring them into her experience until they became more natural to her than the old feelings of anger.

It is important to replace old, unwanted and unneeded energy with energy that is healthy and supportive, otherwise the old energy will return to fill the space. It is important that the client be the one to choose the color and or type of energy to bring in as it is this person's higher self and spirit who knows what is best for them.

This session was a gift for me because it forced me to rethink the paradigm that I had been believing. Was it really possible for someone to allow the space for true healing to occur without diving into the feelings and sinking into the pain? This client had spent years in therapy feeling and expressing her pain, but she wasn't willing to do that anymore. Not only did this process release her anger, it moved her into a deep space of peace and well being. This presented a very exciting possibility. My opening to this door provided me a more expansive belief about healing that I could share with others.

From working with a variety of people, it appears to me that there must be a willingness to give expression to any feeling that arises. If there is judgment about expressing feelings or judgment about which feelings are "right "or "wrong" to express, then these judgements, or the inner critical voice, must be spoken to. When the critic is quelled it is easier for the energetic system to clear itself. As I mentioned earlier, Spirit can only assist us in our healing when we are open and willing. We have free will. If a part of us is refusing or unable to fully bring Spirit in, then that part needs to come into alignment with the intention for healing so that we have all our will present.

Our state of openness and willingness is a reflection of how much we are able to love ourselves and all aspects of ourselves completely. Sometimes a client who has read about past lives, karma, or creating our own reality comes to me voicing that even though mom/dad/sister/brother/uncle abused/neglected/hurt him or her in some way, it is completely forgiven because he or she understands that it wasn't the other person's fault or intention to hurt them. But healing doesn't happen on an intellectual level. Forgiveness must go beyond the mind and permeate every cell.

If the body is in agreement with a notion it will show it, if it is not it will show that as well. In fact, understanding, when used to avoid feeling, can even hinder the healing process. Healing comes from the heart and moves through the body on a cellular level. Healing comes when every cell lets go of the pain and receives truth, love and compassion.

When we try to avoid feeling and carry judgement about ourselves (like it is not ok to be angry or to speak feelings of revenge, hate, etc. because it is not "nice" or "spiritual"), the ability to love the self becomes completely blocked. The amount of blockage in the body on a cellular level is a direct reflection of the pain and suffering that we perceive we have endured, and are still enduring. The more severe the abuse, the stronger the feelings will be. In this work, expression without judgement allows the energy to leave the cells. Expression does not mean wallowing in old murky waters or blaming others. It just means being honest. I believe that once it is accepted that the expression of any emotion is in perfect harmony with God and healing, then that emotion or energy can be released from the body without going into the drama of the event, and sometimes without even having conscious awareness of the trauma.

From countless client sessions I have seen that the willingness to heal allows healing to occur more quickly and easily. Willingness is the key. When clients first come they ask, "How long will it take for me to ....?" My answer always is that it depends upon their willingness to feel, experience, know, release and receive whatever is needed for their healing. Spirit wants us to let go of old baggage and be who we truly are, but Spirit can only assist us as far as we are willing to be assisted. We have free will. Our will cannot be superseded by spirit. If we want healing in a certain area of our lives but say, "I don't want to feel pain, or look at my mother/father issues," Spirit's hands are tied and we can only be helped in a limited way. It is when we are willing to step out of our own way and trust Spirit that the door opens and we are fully able to receive all of the gifts that God/Goddess has for us.

Soul Contracts

The Process

The reader may wonder What is this spiritual hypnosis process? Is it safe? Is this an okay thing to do? Could evil spirits come in and take over? Can I really connect with the spirit of my loved ones and visit past lives? Are past lives even real? I can only answer these questions from the point of my personal experience and the experiences that others have shared with me.

I would first like to say a word about hypnosis. There are many different types of inductions which produce trance states. A trance may be very light and simply induced by watching a movie. If you have ever experienced emotion and gotten "caught up" in a movie, you were probably in a light state of trance. The mind is very suggestible in this state, which is one of the reasons why TV advertising works so well. Trance states can also be quite deep, where the person is so relaxed that they are unaware of, and cannot recall what is being said to them. Yet, while there is no conscious memory in this deep state, the subconscious mind remembers everything that occurs and will respond to suggestions that are given. These suggestions must be in alignment with the client's value system in order for them to work. For example, if the hypnotist gave his client the suggestion to rob a bank, a law-abiding citizen would not be affected by the suggestion. If, however, the client was wanting to rob a bank, the suggestion could cause the client to put that thought into action. Spiritual Hypnosis work occurs in a medium trance state where the mind and body are relaxed, yet the mind consciously aware of everything that occurs in the session. The client can communicate during the session and remember what occurred when the session is complete.

What I do is hypnotherapy. I received the basis for the work from the trainings I have done with David Quigley. Yet several years ago I began to feel that there was something missing from the statement, "I am a hypnotherapist."

I teach and acknowledge that I work only as a guide in the healing process. The healing and "magic" that happens comes from Spirit. There is a force greater than the personality, ego, and learned techniques at work here. I have no attachment to what label is put on this force because, to me, it is all one and the words are just something we need for communication. I use whatever words my client is comfortable with including, Higher Self, Spirit, God, Goddess, Universal Energy or Source. Because I work intentionally with Spirit, and because I want my clients to understand that this is not something I am doing to them, but rather a way in which they can connect and receive information and healing directly from Higher Self, I have chosen to describe my work as Spiritual Hypnotherapy or Spiritual Hypnosis.

The "process" of this work is very simple and natural. Take a moment and recall a time in your own life when you felt confused about what to do in a situation. Maybe you had forgotten someone's name, or misplaced an item. If you allow yourself to recall that situation, you might remember that the harder you tried to figure out what to do, to remember the forgotten name, the location of the lost item, etc., the harder it was to remember. You may have felt that your thoughts were "making you crazy" as they circled around in your head. Or you may have felt "foggy." Then perhaps you forgot about the issue for a moment while you were driving, taking a shower, or washing dishes. In that moment, like magic, the answer to your problem clearly came to you. You may have responded with a, "Now why didn't I think of that sooner!" or, "I remember her name!" or an "Of course, that's where I left it!!" Where did this information come from? After all, you had searched for it, focused on it, and tried very hard to think of the answer. Why was it that when you stopped thinking, the answer came? Was the answer your own thought? If so, then why didn't you think of it when you were trying? Or, is it possible that this thought came to you from your Higher Self, God, an angel or a spirit guide? The answer is yes. Yes, could be any of these or something else. The point is that when we allow the critical mind to relax we become open to receiving information. This openness and receptivity is the basis of the Spiritual Hypnotherapy process.

If you like, you can experiment with this process by using the following simple technique. Find a space that feels safe and nurturing to you. This must be a quiet place where you will not be disturbed by people, pets, or the telephone. You may either lie down or sit, whichever is most comfortable. It is often best to sit on the floor against a wall or in a chair where your spinal column can be straight and supported. It is important that you have a clear intention for what you would like to do at this time. Your intention could be to connect with a loved one who has died, or to gain insight into a challenge that you are facing in your life. Whatever it is, be as specific as you can about what you would like to do or to know. It could be something like, "I want to know if you forgive me for not being there when you died," or

"I want to know if you are okay where you are," or "I feel like so-and-so and I have had a past connection. I would like to know what that was about." Or maybe, "I am so confused about taking or not taking this new job," or "Should I move to Cincinnati?"

When you are clear with what you want, close your eyes and take in some nice deep breaths. You might try this simple breathing technique: Concentrate on your first breath as you slowly inhale through your nose and then slowly exhale through your mouth. Repeat this process until your mind and body feel calm and quiet. The breath is a powerful tool that can take you deep into that place of healing, wisdom and knowing. Imagine yourself sinking deeper and deeper into a place of relaxation and safety. Deeper and deeper into a place of wisdom and knowing. As you imagine yourself safe and relaxed, you can easily begin to count down with each exhale. 10 - 9 - 8 -7- etc. Allow yourself to be as open as possible to whatever images, sounds, colors, smells, or feelings come to your attention. Allow your consciousness to go, without criticism, deeper into whatever comes to you and ask for whatever it is that you wish to know. The message can come in any way, in any form. The most important thing is to be open, to release control, and to be willing to receive whatever is there.

This is a simple outline of the process. Some individuals are able to access past life information or connect with spirit very easily. For others, this process may end in frustration, sleep, or thoughts about what to fix for dinner. Whether or not you are able to access the information you desire on your own is no indication of how spiritually evolved you are. Finding a trained facilitator who can guide you in this inner journey is most valuable. Often when an upsetting emotion such as sadness, grief, guilt, or anger is attached to the subject our subconscious will not take us into that place alone. One of the beautiful things about being human is that the love and support we share with each other is so extremely healing. Sometimes we need the support of someone in order to let go and feel our feelings. Sometimes we need someone whom we can trust and who has the skill of working with the inner world to guide us on that journey. This is true for everyone, no matter where they are on their path.

When I facilitate a Spiritual Hypnosis session I do so in a very specific environment. First, I have the client lay on a copper-grid bed surrounded by crystals. This bed makes it easier to connect with Spirit and keeps the client's energy field clear and free of outside contamination. Crystals impart an energy of their own and, while they enhance the work, they are not necessary.

If the client agrees, I do hands-on energy work during the trance induction. The systems I draw from to do this are called Reiki and Omega. Doing this hands-on work helps the client's and my energies to blend, as well as allows me to bring through the healing energy of Spirit. This blending creates a sense of safety for the client and enables me to be more aware of, and sensitive to, his or her process. The trance induction also involves guided imagery, a verbal count down, stating the intention for only the highest good of the client and progressive relaxation. I also state the intention for communication with Higher Self and spirit guides. Communication with the Higher Self includes a statement about the issue the client is seeking clarification or healing on. This is an invitation to all those in the spirit world who love and desire the highest good for the client to assist with the process. I also include a statement of willingness for the client. This affirms that the client is willing to receive and release whatever may be necessary for this work to be accomplished. I ask my clients to bring in a white light, or light of any color they wish, and surround themselves with this light. I ask them to hold the intention that this light keep them safe, allowing only that which is for their highest good and healing to enter. I hold the intention for myself, the client, and the room to be filled with this light.

At the completion of the induction I remove my hands from the client's body so that my energy does not distract the client from their process. I do, however, work above the body, in the client's energy field, using Reiki, Omega, crystals, and sometimes sound. At this point the session becomes interactive, and through verbal communication I act as a guide, asking questions and assisting the client to receive the desired healing.

When there is communication with a soul that is not embodied, I use my body as an antenna to help facilitate the communication. I sit at the client's head with my right hand about three inches above their forehead, palm down and my left arm, in a comfortable position in front of me, bent at the elbow, with the palm up. When I do this my intention is to be a clear, empty channel so that the energy of the spirit is able to come through and communicate with the client. I began to do this without understanding why. Later I was told, by a Psychic that this did assist with spirit communication.

At the conclusion of a session I go over the important events that happened and have the client give thanks to Spirit for this learning. The client keeps the healing energy from the session within the body's cellular memory where it may be accessed as needed or desired.

Section II

The Veil
Between Worlds

Every person, all of the events
of your life
are there because you have
drawn them there.
What you choose to do with them
is up to you.

Richard Bach

Recognizing Past Life Connections

Love is a fruit in season at all times, and within the reach of every hand.   Mother Teresa

Is love really the answer? It seems to me that it is. When a person is willing to look at a relationship with another, regardless of how painful that relationship may be, there is always love at the core. This love may have to do with the present lifetime, it may be a memory from a past lifetime, a spirit connection, or a combination of all three. Even if we do not remember or want to accept this love, when we are willing and courageous enough to look deep enough we can always find it.

A strong feeling of love, mistrust, fear, hate, compassion, or other emotion for someone in this present-day life can be explored to see if its roots lie in a present-day situation, a past life, or both. If the feeling makes sense to us in this life because of the relationship we have with the person, then at least part of it has to do with this lifetime. But, if the feelings seem incongruent, illogical, or even crazy, they are most likely rooted in a past life. For example, we may wish to leave an abusive relationship, yet, in some peculiar way, feel bound to it. We may fear that a certain person will hurt or betray us and even though there may be no evidence to support this fear, it still exists. We may find ourselves with a compulsion to "save" people who do not want or need saving. They may even use our well meant attempts to care for them as a way to continue dysfunctional behaviors. There are numerous "could be" scenarios and many possible sources. These feelings may come from our own childhood challenges. They may reflect aspects of us that need healing, they may exist as a result of past life experiences, or as a combination of the aforementioned. The key is to find the core.

So how can we recognize when a past-life connection is involved? Look closely at your life. Do you normally find yourself acting logically, but this one relationship seems to make you act in ways that feel unhealthy or crazy and there doesn't seem to be a thing you can do about it? Or do you feel an especially strong connection or attraction to someone for no apparent reason? Or perhaps you have experienced an immediate repulsion or distrust for someone. Have you ever felt an unusual familiarity with someone that you've just met? Or, maybe you've felt like you've known a person before. These are all signs that there could be a past-life soul connection. As you read this book, perhaps some of your own past-life connections will become clear to you.

My interest in, and awareness of, soul connections and contracts has come about through my personal life experiences. My study of energy systems, daily prayer, and a willingness to be of service have opened my awareness to God and the teachings of my spirit guides, and have guided me into a deeper understanding of soul contracts and connections.

Spirit Communication and Reincarnation

My own beliefs about spirit guides, our own inner wisdom, reincarnation, and our ability to communicate with those who have passed over began when I was a young girl. I was born into a Roman Catholic family, but I was never a "good" Catholic. Even as a child, the church's concept of heaven and hell didn't make sense to me. I could not understand how a God who is all-forgiving and merciful could condemn someone to eternal hell with no possibility or opportunity to ever grow or make changes. I remember thinking that I could not condemn anyone to such a sentence, so I questioned how God, who was so much more loving and merciful than myself, could do so. This questioning upset my parents and caused a visit to the local parish where a priest told me that I didn't believe that there was a hell because I was afraid I was going to go there.

I also questioned the belief that each of us has only one life. I was convinced there must be an explanation for why some people who seemed so good suffered in poverty and illness, while others who seemed cold and uncaring enjoyed health and abundance. Since the church was unable to help me in my quest for answers to these questions I began to think about and explore the possibility of past lives.

I did the best I could to make my thoughts fit into the teachings of my family and church, thus I decided, that the "one life" the church taught was the one life of our spirit, and our spirit could wear many bodies. The more I questioned and searched for answers that made sense to me, the less being Catholic worked in my life and I left the church at age seventeen. At this time, I became fascinated by ancient legends telling of gods, goddesses and spirit forms appearing and communicating with human beings. My attention was also captured by stories of appearances of angels and saints within the last century. Information about séances and people who professed to speak with the "dead" also interested me, but I was too afraid to get involved or attend any such gatherings. I did, however, gain a reputation for being quite good with the Ouija board.

Though I continued my search, it wasn't until I discovered Alchemical Hypnotherapy in 1985 and received my first past life session that I was actually able to experience living a past life. Even though the session took place many years ago, I can still clearly remember reexperiencing that life in ancient China. I never had been especially interested in China, but during that session the country and the people were as vivid to me as if I had just returned from a visit there.

As I began facilitating sessions with clients, I was presented with increasing evidence that not only were past life memories and communication with the "other side" a reality, but that they were just as real (or maybe more so) than the physical world. In sessions, many of my clients contacted relations or friends who had just died or who had passed on years earlier. Several things convinced me that these contacts were real. Often clients, came to see me because they were experiencing guilt, grief or stagnation in life as a result of unfinished business with someone who died. After communicating with and receiving forgiveness from the spirit during our session, they would report feelings of deep love, release and freedom. Often the spirit was also wanting to resolve this conflict and we were thanked for making this opportunity available. An energy release would occur, enabling the spirit to move on and go into the Light. On occasion, clients also received information about the deceased person that was not previously known to them. When this information was checked with family members, its accuracy was confirmed. Finally, when a client was communicating with a spirit I would often feel a tingling sensation and experience "goose bumps" on my arms and legs. Sometimes I would experience a cold wave of energy throughout my body, and sense the presence of someone else in the room. Often my sense of this presence would immediately be followed by either the client's initial connection with the spirit or an important part of the communication. One such session involved a client who came to me for the purpose of exploring his lifelong feelings of abandonment.

Bill, as I will call him, had already experienced several years of traditional therapy. This therapy helped him gain insights into his relationship with his mother, where his issues appeared to stem from. He discovered that even after his mother's death he was unable to release her and resolve his issues, in fact, his feelings had intensified. Bill needed to "reprogram" his conscious and subconscious tapes which still contained everything he was told as a child by his parents and other authority figures. Bill was still playing these out of date tapes in response to present-day situations.

During our session, Bill was able to connect with the spirit of his mother. Among other things, she told him how unhappy she had been during her pregnancy and how she had attempted to abort him. She had felt trapped in an abusive marriage and had blamed the baby. Although she eventually left Bill's father and had come to love her son, the scars from this early life experience remained with Bill. This was new information for him. However, insight alone does not heal. During the session Bill was assisted in creating a new prebirth, birth, and infant memory tape. In his new memory he was wanted, cherished and loved. In this process he also imagined releasing the old feelings of not being wanted and saw himself, in the present, accepting the love and friendship he wanted so much. After doing this he was able to forgive his mother for how she had treated him. He was able to feel compassion for her life. She was thankful for this and told Bill that she had been hanging around him, waiting for him to do this healing. She was now released of her guilt and able to move into the Light. Bill hugged her just before she left. He cried and shared that he felt more tenderness and love from her now than he had ever experienced when she was alive.

After our session, Bill called his aunt and checked out the information he had received with her. She admitted that when his mother learned she was pregnant she was very upset, and had resented the baby throughout her pregnancy and during his early infancy. The aunt said that Bill's mother had confided in her but never spoke of this openly; in fact, she went to great lengths to prevent Bill from ever finding out. This is a profound example of how our feelings affect others, even when we are careful and attempt to hide the truth. Our emotions have a magnetic energy that is stronger than words. And even though an individual may not be consciously aware of these feelings, they are affected by them on a cellular level.

The confirmation Bill received from his aunt was powerfully validating for both he and I. His willingness to open to his emotional pain and pursue his healing process paid off. Today, Bill is a far happier and more self confident man, and he is involved in a loving relationship.

Other convincing evidence has resulted from work concerning past lives. Sometimes a client who had absolutely no belief in reincarnation will spontaneously regress to a time period of which she or he had no previous conscious knowledge. When this occurs, both myself and my clients are made aware of how each lifetime is an opportunity to learn specific lessons which offer growth and expansion of consciousness. This explains why some clients, despite their dedication to inner work and therapy, find some issues impossible to resolve until lessons from past lifetimes are fully integrated into their present life. Today I see this as reclaiming the parts of our soul selves from which we were energetically separated, and bringing them home so that we can be whole. This reclamation offers us more energy and ability to live in the present and create the kinds of lives that we desire.

Soul Contracts

Through the Veil

A friend of mine who recently lost his wife to cancer has two young daughters. He told me how, one evening, one of the little girls was crying and missing her mommy so much that she could not be comforted. Through hypnotherapy he was able to have her "imagine" going to a safe place where she and mommy could meet. Not only was she able to do this, but she felt comforted by her mommy and was able to "hear" words that her mommy spoke to her.

Is this all imagination? From my experience, I think not. My belief is that the girl's mommy really did visit and comfort her. Often when we are close to someone, especially when there is a need, such as that of a child for a parent, the spirit makes the choice to stay close by.

My friend now does a Spiritual Hypnotherapy process with his daughters whenever they need or want to "talk" with mommy. Spirit can communicate with us when we are open and this process allows us to still the mind and open our hearts and awareness so that we are able to experience those who live in the spirit world. It appears that the more we are aware of and are willing to communicate with spirit, the thinner the veil between the physical and non-physical worlds becomes. Not only can we in the physical body receive helpful information from the spiritual realm, we can reciprocate and offer this healing opportunity to spirit.

Several years ago, a student of mine was able to connect with a young nephew who had died at fourteen years of age. We were doing some work in that place where spirit dwells when this boy came up and contacted him. The boy, needing help to move through some pain, had been waiting for his beloved uncle to die and move into the spirit realm where he could help him. Now, with this process, he was able to receive what he needed and was free to move into the Light without his uncle having to die. He said, "I am so happy that you are doing this! Now I can move on!" Many, many times in doing this work, the spirit will express a deep gratitude for the client's willingness to enter this space, communicate and do healing work.

Just this past week my husband, Tom, awoke to tell me of an unusual dream. It was one of those dreams in which you can't tell if you are awake or dreaming. He was lying on our bed when he heard someone out on the balcony. He could see the shape through the curtains and so he asked, "Who's there?" It happened to be a young man whom we had foster-parented several years ago. I will call him Edward. Although he had done much good work, was away at college, and seemed to be doing his best ever, Edward had committed suicide. In this "dream" he asked Tom for help because someone was after him. Even while relating it next morning, Tom felt upset by the dream. He felt that Edward's soul was calling to him. Because of the work I do, I naturally suggested doing a session so that Tom could communicate with Edward. In the session, Tom entered into a space where he felt Edward's energy. Edward told him that he wanted our forgiveness for what he had done and said that he loved us. Tom replied that we had forgiven him and that we loved him as well. At this time, Tom felt a very strong, vibrating energy running through his hands and throughout his entire body. Tom said, "Edward's energy is very powerful."

I asked if Edward was willing to share with us why he had taken his life. He was willing, and told Tom that he had been doing poorly in school, but that this was not his reason. He had been spending more and more time out in the wilderness and was feeling very connected with Spirit. He shared that his drop in grades was a reflection of the fact that his spirit was already leaving. He said that he made the decision to take what he had learned and then return in service for healing on the planet. He said that he left with this intention and it was not related to fear.

Near the end of the session, Tom sensed that a cord was wrapped around his own heart. He was told that this had been present for protection, but now that time was over and the heart needed to be freed if Tom's energy was to flow completely through his body. When Tom said that he was willing for this to happen, a spirit guide came in and released the cord. Tom sensed the energy flowing through him and his heart felt more open than ever before. Edward seemed pleased with this occurrence and began to fade away. It appeared that he had come to Tom to motivate him to do this work. It seemed like his gift for the gifts that Tom had given him.

When I related this story to a friend, she commented that when Edward spoke of returning to serve the planet, he may not have meant returning in a physical body, but rather working to serve through the spirit realm. My body tingled when she said that, so it feels true to me. Edward's gentle nature certainly lends itself to that possibility.

The question is: Is this fact or fiction? Again, from personal experience and from sharing this work with others, I have no doubt that soul connections are real. Often when a spirit enters the space where a client and I are working, my body responds with chills and goose bumps and my hair stands on end. Clients often respond in a similar manner, or they may experience deep, sometimes overwhelming emotion, or a strong feeling or sense that a person is with them in spirit form. This, plus the fact that information imparted by spirit has often been found to be true, gives me full confidence that the spirit world is very near and within communication's reach.

The Story of Byron

I am convinced, through my personal work and work with others, that it is the intention and thoughts we hold at the time of death that imbed themselves in our very cells and come back with us when we return to a physical body. I used to think that the best way to leave this body would be to die peacefully in my bed. From my experiences with Spiritual Hypnotherapy work I have come to know that it doesn't matter how we die, quietly or traumatically, what matters is where our energy is when we make that shift into spirit. If we die with fear, resentment, anger, guilt or shame, we carry this turmoil into our next incarnation. If we take the feelings of peace, forgiveness and self love to our death, we incarnate with that peace even if the last body died in a traumatic way.

It is good to know that a soul who has left in confusion, guilt, or sorrow can be reached after death, and healing can occur. Through this work, it is as easy to connect with someone who died a long time ago as it is to connect with someone who has recently made the transition. I hold the vision that there will come a time when each of us who passes has someone who is willing and able to connect with us and that this person will make certain that we are alright and where we need to be.The story of my client Marie and her nephew Byron is a wonderful illustration of this work.

Marie came to see me for a session shortly after her

nineteen-year-old nephew, Byron, was killed in an auto-mobile accident. Byron had been attending college and doing all of the "right" things. He was popular, smart, and his future looked bright until the unexpected head-on collision happened. Of course, his whole family was in shock. Marie had done spirit work with me before and wanted to see if she could gain some understanding of this tragedy. Her first statement to me was, "I know that he's alright. He's spirit. It's the rest of us that need help."

My response was that Byron may be alright, but not necessarily. Often when a soul is taken so abruptly, without time to prepare for death, there is confusion. The soul may not even realize that the body is dead. I suggested that Marie might wish to locate Byron by going into a trance state and entering that place where spirit lives. She was very willing to do this. As she let go and allowed her body and mind to relax, she became aware of Byron. The following is a partial transcription of the session.

"I don't understand what you're doing, but it's very cool!" said Byron when she found him. He had been killed instantly in the collision. Moments before the accident he was driving his truck along a sunny Arizona highway, then suddenly he was looking down upon his broken body and his grief-stricken family. He was scared, confused, and didn't know what to do.

"What can I do for you?" Marie asked. "I just want my body back!" came the reply. "This wasn't supposed to happen! I like that body!" Byron had been very close to his mom and was crying because he had never wanted to cause her such pain. Marie witnessed his suffering and asked for others who had gone before to come and comfort him. A great, silent, peaceful presence sur-rounded him. Next his great grandmother, whom he had never met in the physical world, came. Such a gentle spirit, she took his hand and told him that he needed to trust. He wanted to trust her so much. He could feel her love for him. Next, a man, who Marie did not recognize, came in and identified himself as Sally's dad. Marie did not know who Sally was. He said that he had loved Byron dearly and now was here to comfort him. Finally, a young man appeared who said, "This place isn't bad once you get used to it. You'll like it here."

Byron began to relax, to feel the caring of these spirits and realize that he had passed through the thin veil which separates the physical realm from the spirit realm. As he began to fill with light, his fear dissipated and he realized that his family was suffering so much partly because they sensed how terrified he was. Now that he was feeling safe and loved he knew that they would sense this and it would help them with their grief.

Byron gave messages to Marie for his mother and his father. He told Marie to tell his grandfather that he wished he could just give him one more hug. At this time he realized that spirits can visit in dreams, so he added, "Tell grandpa that whenever he feels hugged in his dreams to know that it's me. Tell grandma that, too." His girlfriend had broken up with him just weeks before. He sent her the message that this was not about her and added, "This is an old cliche, but it is true: It is better to have loved and lost than never to have loved at all. Thank you for giving me the opportunity to have experienced love in this way. I love you and I always will." He told his parents that he was happy they were having his body cremated and the ashes scattered at a place called Hidden Lake. Then he was finished. He said that he would be sending them light and love from where he was. He was feeling the excitement of being in this new home with these souls who loved him. He waved goodbye, and Marie watched him disappear into the Light.

You might ask, "But how do you know this is real?" I can answer that question through these examples: Marie did not know of the decision for cremation nor of this particular lake. After the session she called Byron's mother and found that these were the exact plans that his parents had made. Marie had no knowledge of who Sally or Sally's dad were. When she asked her sister about this she was told that Sally was her sister's best friend. Sally's dad was a very close family friend who loved Byron like his own grandson. He had died three years prior. It is also interesting that after the session Byron appeared to three family members. These "visitations" were positive experiences. Marie flew to Phoenix for the funeral. When she shared this information it brought peace and healing to family members and friends. While sharing the experience Marie realized that the "silent, peaceful presence" that came through was the presence of God.

What about the statement, "This wasn't supposed to happen?" As I was writing about this incident, it came to me that Byron's spirit had agreed to this assignment before coming into the physical plane. During the session it was clear that both his parents and others would gain peace and strength from having to experience this loss in their lives. When Marie returned from the funeral she told me how it didn't make sense to her that Byron was surprised by his death. She said that he had talked to some friends the morning of his death and told them, "If I don't see you on Saturday night go and visit my parents, they will need to talk to you." To his sister's best friend he said, "Take care of her, she's going to really need a sister," and in a card that he wrote that day, celebrating his mother's birthday, he wrote, "I hope that I will be here to give you a card next year." This was crossed out and followed by, "Why did I write that?, of course I'll be here." From these incidents I can only suspect that the spirit was aware of the agreement but the nineteen-year-old personality did not remember it.

This story shows us how even the death of someone we love can be a gift for our own awakening. It appears that Byron could have made a contract with members of his family to assist them in their growth and understanding through his departure. The more experience I have with Spirit the less separation I see between the two worlds.

Soul Contracts

Exploring Soul Connections

If you are interested in exploring past life soul connections, or connecting with the spirits of those who have passed on, I highly recommend working with a hypnotherapist trained in spiritual work. (Please refer to the appendix at the back of the book for more information.) Without a guide you may find your mind wandering or relaxing into sleep. An experienced guide can gently help you to keep your focus and enter into the place where your cellular memories are stored. There is often some fear associated with retrieving past life memories. This may come from the anticipation of what might be, or from the fear of remembering an actual traumatic incident. A knowledgeable guide helps to create the safety necessary to enter into healing, and can provide you with valuable insight. Also, an experienced guide will assist you with completing communication, bringing healing into the situation, and releasing cellular energy that no longer serves you.

Your guide may direct you to do a body scan to either verify a clear energy field or locate any remaining energy that needs to be cleared. While in the trance state it is easy to imagine looking at or feeling each cell of your body. You are easily able to move from the top of the head down to the tips of the toes and notice any energy cords that do not belong. You can then release the energy cords which bind you to others and clear yourself of any contaminated energy. Once these places are clear you can invite any parts of yourself that left to come back home and fill these spaces. This process enables you to reclaim your personal power, live in wholeness, and gain access to all of your energy. Often, a client will feel an actual physical shift in the body when the lost part or parts are called home. A vibrational and emotional shift is also common. You may wish to have this information recorded, either written or taped, so that you can refer back to the spiritual guidance you received. For more on this subject please refer to the chapter on forgiveness, beginning on page seventy-nine.

Connecting with a departed soul on your own may be easier than attempting past life healing. One way to do this is to take a picture of the departed (if you have one), a letter, or anything that either belonged to or reminds you of this person, and put it on a table by your bed. Set your intention that tonight you desire to communicate with this one. You may use the exercise on page seventeen at night as you lie in bed. Only this time, as you count down, imagine yourself going to a special place where your souls can connect. This might be a favorite spot where you used to meet, a special dream temple, or anywhere that feels right to you. Though you may fall asleep, your intention and openness can enable the spirit to connect with your consciousness in the dream state. Before beginning this journey, set your intention to remember the dream. Have a pen and paper by your bedside so that you can record key points of the dream as soon as you awake, even if this is in the middle of the night. It is best to record the information as soon as possible because even very vivid, "I'll always remember this!" dreams can be easily lost.

I have used this technique successfully myself. About two months after a dear friend died, he came to me in a dream that was like no other dream I have ever had. It was a very clear and physical experience. We sat together and I could hold him in the same way that I can hold a living body. It was a powerful and loving experience. He told me that he had to move on and do the things that he had to do. He said that he had come to say goodbye in this way so that we could be together this one last time before he left. I will never forget that experience. It was several months later when I read that these special, physical dreams are one of the ways in which spirit is able to communicate with us.

Soul Contracts

Section III
Contracts Between Souls

Your friends will know you better
in the first minute you meet
than your acquaintances will know you
in a thousand years.

Richard Bach

Introduction

Often we hear about soul mates. Many people read about, take workshops on, and go searching for their soul mate or twin flame with great zeal. They are driven by the idea that a certain person will fulfill all of their desires. Maybe this is true, but this is not what I am talking about when I speak of soul connections.

Soul connections can show up in many different forms and may cover a broad age range. My belief is that when our hearts are open to allowing soul connections into our lives they occur naturally. "Coincidence" unites souls who have contracted to come together in this lifetime. It appears that souls come together to help each other evolve. This is why some of the strongest soul connections can carry us into our deepest places of pain and fear and into our deepest places of love and transformation.

We have the free will to recognize the energy of a soul connection and learn from it, or to deny the experience and move away from it. Those with whom we have these connections and contracts may be in our lives for extended periods of time, or they may pass briefly by. It is not the time, but the lesson that is important.

The question often asked is "How can I recognize a soul connection?"In the pages that follow I will share with you stories of soul connections. Some are from my personal experience and some I have known through my work with others. As you read them, some may feel familiar to you. They may remind you, in some ways, of relationships in your own life or in the lives of people you have known. In these pages you will find clues for recognizing soul connections and contracts in your own life.

Michael

Where there is great love there are always miracles.   Willa Cather

I first became consciously aware of the soul connection phenomenon when I met my friend Michael. Michael had just been diagnosed with AIDS and was, understandably, feeling quite depressed. A mutual friend of ours referred him to me for hypnotherapy work. When Michael sat down for our initial session the first thing he said was, "You work with guides, don't you?" I answered, "Yes," and asked him how he knew. He told me that he saw them. He went on to describe the three guides he saw standing behind me, and was surprised that I didn't see them myself.

As he lay stretched out on the mat before me for his session, I saw a sheet of black energy covering him. I knew that his situation was serious. The session was gentle and I began to feel a deep sense of caring for this man who lie before me. We scheduled a second session for the following week. When the day of our session arrived, Michael was too ill to come to see me, so I went to him instead. This time I gave him a Reiki session. Reiki is a form of hands-on healing that allows the practitioner to channel the energy of Spirit through to the client for the healing of mind, body, and spirit. On the day following our Reiki session, Michael called to inform me that he had been admitted into the hospital with a serious case of pneumosistis pneumonia.

It just so happened that I was face painting at a conference on laughter and play the day after Michael's hospitalization. When the conference ended, I gathered up a large bouquet of stray balloons, bought a pint of chocolate Hagen-Daz ice cream (Michael's favorite), and entered the hospital complete with a brightly painted clown face. Michael was delighted!

After he returned home, I visited him several times a week. I gave him more Reiki energy, we talked and shared parts of our lives. We just enjoyed being with each other. Soon he was faced with the difficult decision of staying where he was or moving back to Arizona with his parents. He very much wanted to do some healing work in his relationship with his father and so he made the decision to move.

I knew that I would go and visit Michael. However, that visit came sooner than I had expected. When I called Michael one Saturday morning a few weeks after his move, I could hear the shakiness in his voice when he answered. He always did his best to be positive, but this time the quiver in his voice gave way to tears. He related how his stepmother had thrown the classified ad section of the newspaper at him that morning, telling him to find another place to live. Michael suspected that she feared having a son with AIDS at home would be bad for her career. While this hurt him, what devastated Michael was the passive agreement of his father.

Michael soon moved into a very small cottage, became quite ill almost immediately, and had to be hospitalized within the month. Since being in the hospital was not Michael's favorite place, and since I was a nurse, his doctor agreed to send him home if I came and cared for him. As I flew to meet my friend I wondered about this situation. Here I was, a married woman with two children at home, flying down to take care of a man whom I had only known for two months. It seemed a bit strange and I couldn't explain it, yet I knew it was the right thing for me to do. Fortunately, my husband respects and supports my need to follow my heart and the voice of spirit.

The week before traveling to Arizona I had taken a medical hypnosis class. The class provided me with more tools, which I packed along. I felt like a doctor with my little black bag stuffed full of things that might save my friend. When I arrived it turned out to be quite a different story. Michael had resumed smoking and was not interested in any of what I had to offer, including the Reiki that he had previously loved to receive. I'll always remember that first night as I lay on a small mat on the floor just outside his bedroom door breathing in cigarette smoke and feeling angry that he didn't want anything to do with the gifts I came ready to give.

In the middle of my "poor me," angry-with-him fit, the "Voice" spoke and said, "If you can't be with him in the way that he needs you, then leave." There was something about the quality of that voice that brought me back to center and made it clear that I had to make a decision. If I wanted to be with my friend I needed to let go of my expectations and be with him in the way that he needed. If I couldn't do that then I had better get on the next plane and fly home. I made the decision to let go and to stay. For years I had been praying to deepen my ability to love without condition, and here I had the perfect opportunity to practice. I cooked for Michael, sang to him and cared for him. We sat on his bed watching hours of old movies, talking, laughing, and crying together. I felt so blessed and so loved by God. I was so happy and thankful to have this special time with my dear friend.

Michael's mother and grandfather visited often. His grandfather was great! He would take us to the hospital for Michael's appointments and after I left he was a wonderful support to Michael.

Leaving him after these two very special weeks was difficult, but I knew that I would return. I was unsure of how I would afford to buy another plane ticket so soon, but I needn't have worried as Spirit took care of that for me. The day after returning home, I was gifted with two tickets. That gift made it clear that I was supposed to be with Michael again soon. I went to see him three weeks later. I stayed for one week this time.

The day after returning home from my second visit with Michael his mother called and said he had suddenly gotten worse and was back in the hospital. At the time I was leading a healing circle for those with AIDS and I had to wait for nearly a week before I could leave. Michael's mom and even his doctor would tell me, "He's waiting for you to come." His mom told me how he would ask, "Is Linda here?" She would say, "No, two more days." He would then turn over and go back to sleep.

During our last visit together Michael had made it clear that he wanted to die at home and had asked if I would stay with him. When I arrived at the hospital he sat up as best he could and tried to get out of bed, but his body, frail and blue with kaposi's sarcoma, would not co-operate. Though he wanted to go home, his family and doctors would not let him leave, and, sadly, I felt that decision was probably best.

I spent the next fourteen hours with my friend. Most of the time we were alone. I talked to him, sang, and stroked his face and hands. I could feel the presence of his grandmother who had died a few years earlier in the room. Michael had been very close to her, and although I had never met her, I had heard stories about her and knew she was here to help him on his journey to the other side. I was thankful for her presence.

One of my favorite sayings is: "If you can't find humor in something, you're taking it too seriously." Even in this situation I had to laugh because whenever the nursing shift would change, the new staff would come into Michael's room to say hello to me or to offer to get me something to eat or drink. Being a nurse myself, I could imagine them in their staff meeting talking about how this patient's friend had flown here from Washington to care for him. They treated me as if I were a saint. I imagined how surprised they would be if they found out that I had known Michael for such a short time and that I was following something that I didn't even understand.

I finally went on a short break to Michael's mothers house. I started out on a much needed walk when, after only a few steps I heard, "Go back." I was enjoying this moment outside in the warm night air, but the voice persisted and I reluctantly turned back toward the house. As I entered the house the phone rang with the news that Michael was ready to go.

Several members of the family came for that last breath. The nurses had Michael's bed cranked to full upright position because he was having so much trouble breathing. I stood next to him, stroking his face and kissing my dear friend's cheek. It was time. As I stood there feeling my love for Michael, I noticed a sheet of white light, over his pelvic area. My eyes followed that light all the way up and out the top of his head where it expanded and then dissipated. As I watched it leave Michael's body, I was filled with utter joy and ecstasy! I had never witnessed spirit leaving before, and the joy was immense! When I looked down at the body, I felt nothing. It could have been a wooden statue sitting there in the bed. It was obvious to me that Michael, my dear friend, was no longer there.

I learned an important lesson from Michael's death. Even though I had been enveloped by great joy at his spirit's leaving, for many days following his death I could not even think of my friend without sobbing as though my heart would break. I never thought I would be able to say his name again without the tears erupting. I remember going to the florist with his mother and grandfather to choose flowers for the funeral. In memory of Michael's love for the Hawaiian Islands, I chose a beautiful bouquet of Hawaiian flowers. It took me by surprise when the woman at the counter gave me a card and told me to write a message on it. What do you write to a dead friend? As I thought of what I would like to say to Michael, I lost control and began weeping so hard that I had to sit down at the desk. Michael's embarrassed relatives left the shop, saying they would meet me in the car.

During this time, it helped me to remember the words of Francis of Assisi as channeled by a friend. Francis said that it is important to allow ourselves to completely feel our feelings. He said that if we do not allow full expression of ourselves, we keep the feelings locked within our cells. Francis advised that whether our feelings be of grief or of joy, we need to feel them completely and let them go. I allowed myself to follow this wisdom and experienced how, even with the joy my spirit felt, my physical body needed to grieve the loss of not having my friend with me on the physical plane.

Until my experience with Michael's death I had little curiosity about past life and soul connections. Now, because of the intensity of this experience, I decided to explore these ideas. Through Spiritual Hypnosis, I found that Michael and I had been together for many lifetimes; in fact, our essence together went back to the beginning of time. I learned that in this lifetime Michael needed to experience being a gay man and I needed to experience a marriage with children. Michael had known that his transition from this lifetime was going to be a difficult one. Because of the love we shared, I had contracted to be with him at his time of death.

To some this may seem like pure fantasy, but it is my truth. Michael and I had grown up on opposite sides of the country. I had moved to Washington and he to Hawaii. Although Michael passionately loved Hawaii and was successful in many endeavors there, when spirit spoke to him he listened. He was told to sell everything and move to the mainland. He had a friend in Colorado whom he decided to go into business with. Though that partnership did not work, it did lead to a relationship with a man named Bill. Bill *just happened* to come from a town near my home in Washington. Michael and Bill decided to move back to this town and shortly thereafter Michael became sick and was diagnosed with AIDS. Although he had never gone to a therapist and wasn't crazy about the idea, when a mutual friend recommended that Michael see me, he did.

From this experience, I believe that when a contract is made, the souls will come together regardless of geographic circumstances. We don't need to search for our "soul mates" or other soul connections. No matter what the time or space, souls who are meant to meet will meet. All we need to do is to hold our heart open and be willing to recognize the connection when it comes. Of course, events will unfold as needed regardless of whether or not we recognize the contracts involved. However, recognizing soul connections can lead to greater understanding and deeper healing.

After Michael's physical death, I could feel the presence of his spirit around me for several weeks. The most memorable event of that time occured when I was called to a hospital to do Reiki on a man, whom I will call John. John had AIDS. He was delirious and not even the medications prescribed by the doctor could calm him. As I walked into the hospital, I asked for Michael's help. When I entered John's room I moved his bed out from against the wall and positioned myself behind him. As soon as I placed my hands on John's head, he completely relaxed. The room became silent as everyone in the room looked at me in awe. I couldn't tell them that Michael was there with me assisting souls who were stuck to John to move into the Light. Soon John was sleeping soundly.

As I left the room, John's partner followed me out. He thanked me for coming, then told me that John was leading an AIDS support group in which several of the members had recently died. When I heard this, it made perfect sense to me that these souls were clinging to him. Sometimes if a person is afraid to die, their soul might cling to someone to whom they feel connected. In this case, that person was John. When this happens the soul needs reassurance that moving on is not only safe, but desirable. Michael's part was to help these souls to realize this so that they could cross over into the Light. I believe that these souls were draining John's already fragile energy system, so when they were removed, John's energy could go back to supporting his body.

Although this was a powerful experience for me, I was not prepared for what happened the following day when I stopped by to check on John. When I entered his room I found him sitting up in bed. He looked right at me and said, "Thank you for being here last night." That shook me. The only time I had ever seen John was the night before. He had his eyes closed, and was thrashing in his bed until the energy work began. Except for the brief moment it took me to walk to his bedside, I was behind him. He was sleeping when I left. So, how did he recognize me? I can only believe that he saw me through his spirit eyes. John recovered quickly and returned home. He continued to lead his support group for several more weeks. He died, peacefully at home, about four months later.

Michael appeared to me, in his spirit form, a few weeks following our visit to the hospital. He came to tell me that he had other things that he had to do. I am thankful for the all the gifts this friend shared with me, especially the awareness of soul contracts and connections. A wonderful example of this awareness recently came into my life. I met a woman who was just married. She and her husband met on an airplane. He had noticed her in the airport and she noticed him noticing her. It just *happened* that by "coincidence" they were assigned seats next to each other. It also is true that even though they both live here in Seattle their families live in, and they were born in, Newport, Rhode Island. They happened to be back visiting at the same time. Coincidence? I don't think so. My guess is that they have a soul connection.

Soul Contracts

Marc

Several years ago my daughter Vicki asked if Tom and I would be willing to consider becoming foster parents for a boy, whom I will call Marc. Marc was in Vicki's class and had to leave his family because he could not agree with their religious beliefs. He had no place to live and was frightened. We had not taken someone in for about six months and were thinking that it was time to stop foster parenting and let our biological family have a year alone together. Our daughter would be leaving home soon and our time remaining seemed precious and short. I also had my hypnotherapy practice in Seattle and, knowing how much time a new foster child requires, felt that it would be too much for me to take on. We did agree that he could come to a summer party at our home and so we met. Although he seemed like a nice young man, I had no desire for him to live with us. Then, as Marc and I were talking on the stair landing in our home, a curious thing happened.

At the precise moment I was going to tell Marc the decision was "No," a friend of his who had briefly dated my daughter walked in. This young man came uninvited. My previous experiences with him had left me feeling that he was an energy "sucker" and could not be trusted. I knew that he had offered Marc a room in his apartment. I liked Marc and the thought of him moving into that situation didn't feel good. As this person, Marc's friend, entered, I didn't have time to think. I only saw the room fade into blackness. At the same time I felt like someone reached in, grabbed my stomach and intestines, and began squeezing them until I said, "Okay, I'll take him! Just let go!" I was overtaken by the experience, the pain stopped, and when I was free I knew that Marc would come and live with us. There had been other times when I had known a young person was to live with us, but none as dramatic as this.

Marc and I had a strong connection from the beginning. We talked about spirit and energy easily and openly, even though he had not previously discussed these concepts with anyone. Our relationship developed into one of caring and trust. Many significant moments occurred, yet three incidents in particular stand out as excellent soul-connection examples.

One night Marc and I were talking in his room. He was propped up on pillows, back to the headboard, and I was sitting crossed-legged at the foot of his bed. The light in the room was dim and we were having a comfortable conversation. All of a sudden Marc said, "I see you as an old man with a beard!" A few moments passed and he said, "Now I see you as an old woman!" From teaching past life regression classes I recognized the exercise of looking into someone's eyes until you can see into their soul and recognize a past life personality. It is said that the eyes never change. Even though I had used this exercise in class many times, I myself had never "seen" someone's face change form.

As I looked across at Marc and listened to him talking about how he was experiencing my face changing, this phenomenon took place for me as well. All of a sudden I was looking into the face of a beautiful young black man, and it scared me. It scared me so much that I closed my eyes. Then I asked my spirit, "Let me see this one more time." I opened my eyes, and for an instant I saw the image once again before it vanished. I felt a bit shaken by the experience and I didn't understand its meaning. I told Marc what I had seen and he asked, "If I was beautiful, why were you scared?" Thoughts of black magic and sorcerers raced through my mind but nothing made sense, so I only said, "I don't know." And I didn't. I was perplexed. I found it interesting that Marc, a white boy who felt such a strong connection with the black culture, came to me in a vision as a black man.

The second event happened when Marc told me that he was planning to sign up for the army. Desert Storm was in progress and he thought that he would like to join the armed forces and go to war. I have always encouraged my children to pursue their ideas for life and have been quite open to them making their own decisions. My response to Marc's statement surprised me. I became angry and desperately tried to talk him out of joining the army. I was demeaning about his interest in the military and found myself saying anything I could think of to try and stop him from making that decision. We argued about it. I could not understand the intensity of my reaction, but understand it or not, it was there.

I asked my spirit for guidance in this situation, and the perfect opportunity arose. A student from my hypnotherapy class needed to give a session before she could complete the past life part of the program. She offered to give me the session. I, of course, said "Yes."

During my session I sank deep within and I found myself, a black woman, in a small wooden boat floating down the river. Very soon I came to my village and my son, whom I recognized as Marc, came running up to meet me. (I knew it was him from the eyes. The eyes are the mirror to the soul and during past life regression you can recognize people from your present life through the eyes.) It was a joyous reunion! He was probably about seven or eight years old at the time. We lived in a very loving and peaceful village. A man, who was my friend Michael in this present life (the same person in the last story), also showed up. I believe that he was Marc's father, or maybe a chief at that time. The reasoning for this, you will read in a moment.

Time passed and Marc was about sixteen years old. It was time for a ritual ceremony where he would be taken into the tribe as a warrior. He and I were in a small straw hut together. He was standing and I was kneeling in front of him fastening a beaded belt around his waist. It had what looked like a piece of red horse hair hanging from the center

In the next scene, our village had been attacked. My present time physical body, the one lying on the mat in front of my student, began to shake as I began a deep, uncontrolable sobbing. I could not finish the session. I could not bear to look at what happened. This was very unusual for me because by this time I had received numerous sessions and had never before been unable to come to completion, no matter how painful the session might be. I knew that I would have to return to that place to complete that lifetime. About two weeks later I had the opportunity to do just that.

In another hypnotherapy session I returned to the past life scene after the attack. I found myself walking through the jungle desperately looking for my son. I finally found him, strung up by ropes, quartered and hung in the trees. It was a terrible thing to see. Now I understood why such fear came up when I saw that beautiful black man as we talked that night. My cells were beginning to recall this memory and, because of the intensity of the trauma, a part of me did not want to remember. He was no sorcerer, he was my son. It also made sense why I reacted so angrily when Marc talked about going to war.

There was one more incident that revealed my connection with Marc. Some weeks prior to my session, Marc had been depressed and was experiencing a difficult time. There was nothing I could say or do to ease his pain and so I went, as I often do, for a walk down by the lake. Two years ago, just before his death, my friend Michael had showed me a very old beaded necklace with red horsehair hanging from the center. He collected antiques and told me how this had belonged to a warrior. Although I had no interest in the piece, he carefully took it out of it's box and showed it to me on three occasions. Because of the importance it seemed to hold for him, I took it with me after he died. I put it away and never thought about it until Marc came to live with us. I repeatedly had the feeling that I should give it to him. I shrugged it off. I didn't think that a seventeen-year-old boy would be interested in this rather bedraggled beaded necklace. But that day as I walked by the lake, I actually "heard" Michael's voice say, "Give him the necklace!" I went home, retrieved the piece from it's little box, and took it to Marc. I started out with, "I don't know why, but I'm supposed to give you this." But explanations weren't necessary as his immediate and powerful emotions took over. He loved it! His reaction surprised me. At the time I didn't understand why Marc would feel this way. After my session, however, it made perfect sense. This necklace I had given him was amazingly similar to the belt I had fastened around Marc's waist in that past life. My guess is that there was a matching necklace which I did not notice. Could this even have been the same one? That I didn't know.

After completing that past life in my second session, I told Marc about my experience. We both had tears in our eyes and he said, "It is like I came back to you at the age I left that time so we could complete our relationship." This statement was very moving and I could see how the contract had been made for us to complete this past life's drama in our present life.

This true story shows how past life soul connections, memories and contracts can affect our present-day relationships. It is easy to see how, if left unresolved, these connections can cause illogical and even hurtful reactions. The connection could even destroy a relationship through fear and control rather than strengthening it with love and understanding.

Peter

During my time as a foster parent I made the connection with a young man whom I will call Peter. From the first time we met, both Peter and I felt a strong bond. In fact, at our first meeting Peter thought that he remembered me from his home state of Minnesota. Because of my exploration of soul connections, I suspected that one existed between Peter and I.

Peter had come to us very troubled. He had been abandoned by his biological parents when he was a small boy and had lived in several foster homes. As time went on Peter increased his involvement in the drug culture. He lied, did not come home when he said he would, and could not be trusted. I had done a lot of inner healing work and foster care before this relationship so I was surprised with how difficult the situation was for me. I became depressed and could do very little in my own life. I felt completely co-dependant and crazy as I found myself centering my life around trying to help Peter. I felt drained of energy. No matter what I, my family, or friends did or said I couldn't seem to come out of it. This state continued until I received a hypnotherapy session that shifted the energy circuits. During the session, I imagined talking with Peter. The therapist asked me to look above his body in this vision and connect with his higher self. In the moment that I connected with his higher self, I felt a surge of energy running through every cell of my body. The intensity was such that I felt as if I had been plugged into an electrical socket. Peter's Higher Self spoke to me saying, "This is the energy that you remember. It is not his body or his behavior that you are connected with, it is this energy. You came down here to help each other to learn, but he is not willing to be responsible for himself at this time." Right there I got it. It was as if someone had woken me up from a dream. I fully realized that the connection I felt was very real and I also realized that I did not have to participate in the abuse or see myself as a victim to his behavior. Seeing the greater picture gave me understanding and helped me to disconnect my energy and begin to separate myself from him. I was now free to move forward.

In this session, I saw a movie played out before me. I was shown how each one of us decides what lessons and experiences we want to encounter in order to grow. We make our alliances with others in the spirit world who are willing to help us achieve our goals and then we come down into the physical realm, dress up in these costumes that we call bodies, and begin the play (or the drama). But we forget that we are wearing costumes and that we chose the lessons. Until we are able to see this, we believe the illusion and perceive that these events are happening *to* us instead of for us. Often it seems that these events and the people involved in them are causing our pain and we feel victimized.

From my experience with Peter, I now understood why some people who want so much to get out of an abusive relationship are not able to, even when they see how destructive it is to their lives or their children's lives. The ties that bind us together from the past can be even stronger then those we make in this current lifetime. We can remember the energy of a soul and feel our love and connection to it, but that does not mean that that particular soul has embodied with the intention of following a path compatible with our own.

Despite the shift in energy around my situation with Peter, I began having some feelings of guilt about separating my energy from his. I decided to explore this in another session. In this second session, I was the mother of two children. Our family was very poor and my husband ordered that I should sell one of the children as a servant. I had no choice but to do his bidding, so I sold my eldest, who happened to be Peter. As I saw these events unfold, I received that Peter had been carrying around the issue of abandonment for many lifetimes, and this was the issue that his soul chose to heal in this lifetime. I also was told that it was important that we heal this abandonment issue together because one of my lessons for this lifetime was self love and honor. At death in that past life I made the contract that, if I were given another chance to have him as my son, I would never abandon Peter. I believe this was why I allowed myself to be abused and could not simply walk away from the situation.

Through Spiritual Hypnotherapy I learned that although the spirit connection between Peter and I was very beautiful, it had nothing to do with present life choices or behaviors. I saw that my first and foremost lesson in this was to love myself and honor my life. Now I was able to make the choice to do that. Because I no longer carried the guilt that drove me to try and make things good for him, I was able to honor his life and his choices, regardless of how I felt about them or what I thought would be best. I learned that it is my responsibility to trust that God is in charge, and I do not need to know or understand why the other person is choosing to walk a certain path. I need only be accountable for my life and my choices.

This view may sound self-centered because we are so often told to "do for others." But we must examine *why* we are doing for others. When we express compassion, caring, and assistance to others from a place of clear intention that is not attached to creating the outcome that we want, we exhibit unconditional love. The only life that we have the right to is our own. It doesn't matter how many right, good, loving reasons we have to fool ourselves into believing that we know what is best for someone else. We cannot control anyone else's life or destiny. When we attempt to change someone else's situation we only prolong the lesson for them as well as for ourselves. When we send our energy out to try to live someone else's life, we lose the energy that we need to live our own lives. It is important to watch for signs of this behavior, which we are all prone to. These signs include depression, anxiety, physical ailments, and lack of energy.

I heard a story a long time ago about a woman who prayed vigilantly for many years that her brother would stop drinking. Finally, one day during her prayers an angel spoke to her and said, "You've been doing it wrong." Shocked, the woman asked, "What do you mean, wrong?" The angel then told her to simply send prayers of love and acceptance (unconditional love) to her brother. A few days later her brother called to say that he had made the decision to go into an alcohol treatment center. Whose lesson was this? Did the brother continue his drinking so his sister could gain this gift? What part do our attachments and well-meaning prayers and advice play in another's life?

Kate

Every person, all of the events of your life are
there because you have drawn them there. What
you choose to do with them is up to you.
                                        Richard Bach

One of the joys of this work is knowing that Spirit
is always there guiding the process. The more open you
are willing to be, the easier it is to notice the "voice" of
spirit and the more wonderful life becomes. In my work
and in my teaching "miracles" often occur. One
particularly memorable miracle unfolded while I was
teaching a hypnotherapy class. We were doing the
weekend entitled Etheric Plane Communication. The
techniques taught in this weekend are powerful for
enabling communication with anyone, dead or alive.
This communication allows for understanding and
healing to take place between the client and whomever
is being communicated with. Normally, we give one
session demonstration on Sunday. But, when we walked
into class on Saturday one of our students, Kate,
expressed that she was having severe back pain. Instead
of beginning class in the usual way, I asked the class if
they would like to see how etheric plane communication works in dialogue with the body. Everyone
responded with an enthusiastic "Yes" and so the session
with Kate began.

During the session, Kate shared that when she went into the place within her subconscious and into the center of the pain in her back, she found her brother John. She wasn't very happy about finding his energy there. Yet when one commits to healing and is open to the process, it is often the situations and people we don't want to look at that show up. These are the ones who are the "pain in the neck," back, head, etc. More accurately, they are the ones who we have our energy attached to.

Kate's process was fairly quiet, with much of the work being done internally. Those of us in the room could only guess at what was happening as she lie in front of us experiencing her feelings, which turned out to be of hurt, anger and betrayal directed towards her brother John. Finally, Kate came to a place where she was able to begin the process of compassion and forgiveness for John. As her body began to relax and she started to release the anger she had held, it became clear how not being able to forgive her brother John was disabling her own life and keeping her from living from her center. Kate became acutely aware of how deeply this lack of forgiveness was affecting her life and the way she moved through the world.

During this experience of releasing anger and victimhood, Kate was able to bring in the soft, sweet energy of forgiveness. She was able to breathe this energy into every cell of her body, and as she did so she could feel a shift occurring. When she opened her eyes and returned to her full waking consciousness, the back pain had not disappeared but it was markedly less. Kate had chosen not to disclose revealing facts during her session and so neither myself nor the other students were aware of what her situation with John was.

The miracle of this event lies not so much in the session itself, but in what followed. On the third day following this inner dialogue with her brother, Kate received a letter from him. This is significant because they had not communicated for at least ten years. It is also noteworthy that he began the letter on the very day she signed up for the hypnotherapy class, but did not mail it until the day she had received the session.

Kate later pointed out to me how, in his letter, the only thing John had asked her for was forgiveness. He had been praying for this for a long time. Kate feels that his prayers and thoughts helped to open the space for this session and the healing that followed. She felt that his intention for healing helped guide her spirit to taking these classes. I agree with her. Through this work I have become aware of how we are connected energetically, especially to those we love, and how that connection can and does effect us.

During the next weekend of our class, Kate shared her brother's letter with me. Students were paired up for an exercise and I began to open the envelope. At that moment I received a strong message to go outside and read it in a quiet space by myself. I stepped out and sat on the steps in front of the classroom. As I held the paper in my hands I felt the words touch my soul. (An excerpt from the letter appears below.) I sat crying and feeling the pain in the pages, as well as the pain of others who have been on both sides of this victim/perpetrator cycle,. I was so moved that I asked Kate if she and her brother might allow me to share their story in this book. They both agreed to let me share it and it is their hope, as well as my own, that this soul connection work will be an asset in ending the perpetrator/victim cycle and that it will help bring understanding and the true possibility of healing to pedophillia, a condition that our society considers to be contemptible and untreatable. And so, they share this excerpt from John's letter with you.

Soul Contracts

The reason that I'm writing this letter to you is to say how sorry I am for sexually molesting you when you were younger. There is no excuse for what I did to you.

I never should have touched you in a sexual manner in any way, shape, or form at any time. I want to express to you my deepest level of guilt, remorse, and how truly sorry I am for what I did. I've got a sickness called pedophillia, which is a disease in which I get sexual pleasure from children.

I've had this disease for many years. I want to express my deepest regret for any emotional trauma that you've suffered in the past and for any emotional trauma that you still are suffering to this day. . . .Nothing that happened back then or now is/was your fault in any way, shape or form. Brothers aren't supposed to do these kinds of things to their little, helpless sisters.

I'm now in a group for sexual offenders and I have been for most of the time since I came to prison. It's part of my therapy. I've talked to them about writing this letter to you. They made me realize that because of the suffering that I've caused you to go through all these years that you might not want anything to do with me, that there's just too much pain and suffering that I have caused you to go through. I truly hope and pray this is not the case, but if it is I'll accept your feelings. I dearly miss the special closeness that the two of us used to have, the late night talks and the car rides we used to take to the dock by Chism Park. You have always been special to me.

I hope this letter will start some communication between us about the effects my actions have had on your life. It is hard for me to fully understand and comprehend how my actions have caused suffering in people that I've known. . . . I can only guess what this has done to your life in the sense that I was myself molested by a classmate when I was ten years old. I'm just beginning to understand how this has affected me ever since. . . . I can only imagine it much worse for you to have had it be your own brother as the one who molested you. Someone who you are supposed to be able to look up to. Someone who's supposed to look out for and protect you and love you. Lastly I ask if it is possible that sometimes in the future that I can have your forgiveness.

I know that you can never forget what I did to you when I molested you. If there's anything I can do for you, please let me know.

Love , your brother John

Kate shared that if she had received this letter before we had done the session her response would have been "Fuck you!" and the letter would have been thrown into the garbage without ever being opened. Because of the deep healing that she was able to do, and her willingness to enter into true forgiveness, she was not only able to read the letter, but was moved by it.

Shortly after the letter's arrival, Kate and John's mother passed away. John was briefly allowed out of prison to attend the funeral. Kate had not seen her brother for over ten years and now he stood in front of her, locked in iron shackles. Here, beside their mother's coffin they were able to able to embrace each other and Kate was able to share her forgiveness with John.

I asked Kate if she would be willing to do another session with me to see what past life connections and learning might be a part of the larger picture of this story. She was willing to do this. When we later met for the session, Kate was feeling resistance to finding what this connection might be, but she proceeded with the session.

In the first part of our session, Kate was taken into a field where she was being chased by members of her tribe. She was a Native American man. When we went back in time to find out more about this situation she found that she was a healer, a shaman. The chief's wife and child were in serious danger from childbirth and the chief had called her to save them. As she held the baby in her hands she knew there was nothing that she could do. The child died and the angry chief ordered that she be killed. The chief from this lifetime was her brother today. Kate went to her death in that past lifetime feeling betrayed and angry. She made the decision that she would not use her "magic" again. In that place between lives where spirit lives, Kate saw that the lesson from this life-time was to accept her gifts and accept destiny.

In the next life-time, Kate was a young man of seventeen. Her brother from this life-time was also her brother then. He was nineteen. There was a lot of competition between the boys, and out of anger Kate stabbed her brother in the heart and killed him. The awakening of her cells to this memory was intensely emotional. As she felt the knife sink into his heart, she heard his last words, "I'll get you, you bastard!"

Kate was cast out of the family and left to wander for the remainder of her life. She died, frozen to death, alone in the wilderness. As Kate remembered those events, she could physically feel her hands and feet becoming cold and numb as the freezing occurred. She remembered that her final thought was to never be alone again. At this point in the session, Kate went into that place in between lives, and received a message from her spirit guides. The message was: "You cannot hold hate in your heart. Hate will kill you and your spirit. All of our lessons serve us. You must forgive."

As Kate began to fill the cells of her body with the golden light of forgiveness for herself and for her brother, she began to experience healing, wholeness, and freedom in her body. When we checked in to see if this energy work was completed Kate saw how she and her brother had brought their parents much pain in that life time. The guilt from that life was still held in her body's cellular memory. In the session, she was able to release that energy, and as she did she began to feel the grace of self-forgiveness for that situation enter into her cells, replacing the guilt that had been held there. At this point, I was doing energy work over Kate's body and received a very strong message about self forgiveness.

Often I have heard others say and have even said myself, "It's so much easier to forgive someone else rather than yourself." The message in this is twofold. First, I do not believe that we can truly forgive another without forgiving ourselves. Second, it is so much easier to forgive someone else because of the fear we have of self-forgiveness. If we truly forgive ourselves then we *have* to forgive others which means we must release the victim role. This means we have to step into the full power of who we are. The message that Kate received in her past-life regression, "You cannot hold hate in your heart. Hate will kill you and your spirit. You must forgive," is a very powerful statement. When she heard this, Kate says that "I gathered back my energies as I forgave first my brother, then myself." Forgiveness of her brother was freeing, but forgiveness of herself was the most powerful and healing aspect of the equation. Forgiveness of herself was essential for Kate to feel self-love.

This story again shows how we take the emotions and thoughts that we die with into the cells of our next physical incarnation. We can either choose to act them out again in the present incarnation or choose to become conscious and reach forgiveness, understanding, and compassion for ourselves and others. If we take the unconscious route and act out our hate and revenge, we continue on the karmic wheel of suffering. To me this is what hell is about, and we create it, not God. Through our hate and unwillingness to forgive we do a marvelous job of condemning ourselves. Through forgiveness, we restore our health and well being, reclaim our happiness, and find inner peace.

The Importance of forgiveness

Forgiveness is the final form of love.

Reinhold Niebuhr

The story of Kate and John reveals the importance of forgiveness. Holding on to resentment, anger, guilt, or any other emotion that is connected to our lack of forgiveness towards others or ourselves only serves to hurt us on both the physical and energetic planes. Many issues of lack, such as lack of health, money, success, loving relationship, happiness, and energy may be associated with our lack of forgiveness.

But how do we truly forgive on a cellular level? I'm not talking about "New Age" magical thinking here, but true cellular release. So many times clients have come in with a story that includes some version of, "My mother was an alcoholic and beat me, but I know that I chose her as my mother to learn a lesson. She was abused as a child and did the best that she could with her children so I forgive her." The clenched hand and the subtle tightness of the jaw belie the words that are spoken. Even though the intention is there, until the cells of the body are released of their pain and toxicity, the words are just a sham that attempt to cover the road to true healing. The body never lies.

My belief is that forgiveness can only come when we are willing to allow the cells of our body to open to our feelings, no matter how painful the feelings might be. With this opening we have to be willing to love ourselves enough to allow all of the emotions to come forth, true and free of censorship. These may include some "not very nice" feelings and words. There may be feelings of hate and anger accompanied by thoughts of punishing, mutilating, or even killing those whom we feel have harmed us. Whatever comes up must be allowed expression for true healing to happen. The expression of such feelings may take time or may last for only an instant. We may not even have conscious awareness of the incidents behind our feelings. The release, understanding and forgiveness that comes is all completed safely in our inner world with the help of our guides and higher self. No harm is ever done to anyone on the physical plane. It is by going through this door that we enable all of the stuck emotions to be released from our cellular structure. It is through our willingness to enter this place of healing that we set ourselves and others free.

Many times I have had clients who are afraid that if they express their truth it will, in fact, harm the other person. This is far from the truth. It is when we hold on to unhealed energy that we harm others as well as ourselves. When we release this energy we create space for healing and compassion. For example, imagine that you are angry with your father, yet each time he calls, you try to be pleasant. When you pick up the phone and first hear his voice, you may feel your stomach tighten and your energy contract. Your body is giving you a message. It is expressing the truth. Even if your words are "nice," the energy you feel extends out to your father and on some level he feels your anger. He may respond to the feeling and not your words. He may speak angrily or defensively toward you. This gives you more reason to justify your anger and stay in your victim role. You can tell your friends about how nice you tried to be and how mean he was to you. Your friends may be sympathetic towards you and you may never have to take responsibility for the energy that you put out to him.

When you clear anger and pain from your body by expressing your truth, and come to genuine forgiveness of your father, as well as yourself, you take back your power. Now when you pick up the phone and hear his voice, your energy is clear and the possibility for him to behave differently is created. Your new energy may allow him to relax and come off his defensive guard. This clearing and forgiveness is healing for both you and him. This communication does not need to happen on the physical plane.

Through Spiritual Hypnotherapy we can communicate with someone else in a clear and honest way on an energetic level. When this happens we can connect with the other person's truth in a way that is healing and forgiving. For example, during etheric plane communication, you may find that your father treated you so harshly because he loved you and felt that this is what he needed to do for you to turn out alright. Maybe this is what he learned from his father. In the state of hypnosis you can feel your hurt and anger. You can scream at your father and do whatever you need to do to make sure that he knows how his treatment of you has affected your life. When the anger is fully released you can share with him how you wanted him to be there for you, how you missed him and how much you love him. This complete sharing of all the emotions allows for true forgiveness and healing. Communicating in this way on the etheric plane is often far more powerful than if we attempted to do it in the physical. Because we can express ourselves in whatever way we need, the energy that binds the other person to us can be cleared and we become self-empowered.

We always do this work for our own healing, but when we clear our energy and empower ourselves the side benefit is that we also release the other person. This frees their energy to make other choices. They may choose to move closer to or further away from us, to love us more or become angry because we no longer are willing to have the same dysfunctional relationship with them. We may choose to share our experience of healing and forgiveness with the person involved if they are receptive, but it is good to know that this process can be complete without ever involving the other person directly.

If you have feelings of anger or resentment when I speak of release and healing for the perpetrator as well as the client, you may want to look at your own belief of being a victim. Etheric plane communication takes us beyond the victim/perpetrator cycle and into the big picture where healing for everyone is a delightful thing.

How do feelings and thoughts get stuck in our cells? My belief is that the anger we hold in our cells is in direct proportion to the experiences that created it. What comes forth from us is only a reflection of the abusive experiences that have taken our power and stolen pieces of our spirit. By abuse I am talking here about anything that frightened us, hurt us and kept us from being our authentic, true self. When we can let go of judgement for what is "acceptable" and "unacceptable" for a "good," "spiritual," or "nice" person to feel, we give ourselves the blessing of honesty. Once our cells release the pain held in our bodies, they can begin to bring in a new energy, an energy of healing, grace, and forgiveness. Any parts of us that had to leave can be called back, and we can bring ourselves into wholeness. In shamanism this is referred to as soul retrieval.

I've begun to imagine that our bodies are like jigsaw puzzles. You might remember some time in your life when you were putting a puzzle together and tried to make a wrong piece fit. You might have wanted it to fit and thought, "It looks like it should fit," but if you left it there it would have thrown off the whole puzzle and distorted the picture. That's how it is for us. Instead of being born with our unique puzzle intact we may have incarnated with some of our pieces already missing. They may be stuck in past-life beliefs and dramas which we may not even be aware of. In place of our authentic puzzle pieces we may have jammed in pieces that do not fit. These misfit pieces may have been there for so long that we believe they are our true selves. We may have continued to give away more of our true pieces during our present-day physical incarnation, beginning as early as the time of conception. For each piece that we gave away we might have "jammed in" other pieces from parents, teachers, or others whom we have tried to please. Of course, these pieces never fit quite right. These pieces are a metaphor for our energy and the energy of others.

Why would someone give pieces of themselves away? The answer is simple. For survival. For example, I had a client notice that instead of her own "puzzle piece," her mother's energy was living in the center of her body. Her parents had divorced when she was a young girl, and her father left the family. She was very scared that her mother would also leave and so she sent away her puzzle pieces that had to do with independence and success and tried to make her mother's low self-esteem and fear of failure fit into that part of her. She did this because she was afraid that if she did not bond with her mother in this way, but was instead independent and successful, her mother might become jealous or angry and also leave her.

We originally put these pieces in place to protect ourselves. But why do we become so attached to these feelings that aren't truly ours, even when they don't feel right? I believe we do this because they are often all we remember feeling. We falsely believe that they are who we are. The thought of releasing them can feel scary because we fear that we will lose ourselves. The truth is, we will reclaim our power and our true selves.

Because of the unconscious and cellular nature of such decisions they may be difficult to realize and to locate. Spiritual Hypnotherapy helps the client find the places where another's energy has been taken on, release that energy, and reclaim the piece that was given away. With the client I just mentioned, we released the piece that was her mother's and she called back the piece that was hers. Her piece had to do with personal power and success. She no longer needed to protect her little child-self by keeping her energy subdued so as not to anger her mother. Upon calling this piece back she immediately felt a sensation of completeness in her body. When we bring our pieces back home, we find greater wholeness and healing in our lives.

How long does this process take? It can take one session or encompass several sessions. The amount of energy it takes depends upon the abuse suffered, how strong our attachment to victim energy is, and how willing we are to grasp the bigger picture. When we are willing to look at the big picture and let go of judgement, we can find the parts that we played in the drama. Touching upon times when we have been the persecutor allows us to open the door to forgiveness. When that happens we can let go of judgements and anger towards others and ourselves. Forgiveness does not mean that we condone the actions of those who have hurt us, or condone our own actions, it simply means that we forgive.

When teaching I will often hear, "Maybe the child who is being abused today by his father was his father's abuser in a past life. Maybe he deserves what he's getting." The question then arises, "Should we just let abuse go?" My answer is that it may be true that the victim was the persecutor of yesterday, but now it is time to become conscious and to stop the pattern of abuse. If we do not do this, the karmic wheel of pain and suffering continues. If we do not assist the victim in waking up to the greater picture and moving into healing and forgiveness, then we enable that person to remain disempowered and enmeshed in the abusive pattern. If we do not extend compassion to the persecutor, we support them to continue the same pattern. I need to stress here that forgiveness is not the focus of this work. The focus is to be present, without judgement, so that the client can experience the feelings, release the energy, reclaim the self and heal. When healing happens, forgiveness just happens to be the natural outcome.

It is important to remember that past-life memories are not an excuse for present-life behavior. In other words, "I don't have to make amends because I just found out that you killed me in another lifetime and I'm only giving you back what you deserve," is not what this is about. In becoming aware of the whole picture we become accountable to our spirit to live in our highest integrity.

Soul Contracts

Frederick

Frederick first came to me because of the hate that he felt for his step-sister. Frederick had been in pursuit of a spiritual path for many years and was quite aware of the power of thought, forgiveness, and extending love to others. He had tried every means known to him, but still could not resolve the feelings of hatred that he felt toward this woman. Although their relationship had seen difficult times, he could not think of anything that warranted such intense feelings of hate and mistrust. Here was a man who knew the consequences of holding onto such feelings and yet he felt powerless to release them.

Frederick and I decided to do a past-life regression to find out how his soul and the soul of his step-sister Julie might be connected. The intention was also to release any contracts that might have been made between them. During this regression, Frederick was surprised to find that they had been lovers in a previous lifetime. He had been a woman at that time, and she a man. "She" (the present day Frederick) was very much in love, but her lover, the present day Julie, betrayed her by having many affairs. Their relationship finally ended when the lover killed her (Frederick). The last thoughts as spirit left her body were thoughts of revenge and hatred. These thoughts and feelings were carried on a cellular level into this present lifetime.

When Frederick went into that place where spirit goes between lives, he found that he and Julie's spirits were very connected and that there was great love between them. Frederick's soul had decided that, for it's greater learning about love and compassion, it needed to experience betrayal by a loved one. Although Julie's soul was reluctant to play out this drama, the agreement was made. When Frederick was able to feel the love for this soul and was able to see that this drama was set up for his own soul's growth and learning, he was able to release the energy of anger and revenge that he was carrying. For the first time, he was able to enter into a place of true forgiveness and harmony with his step-sister.

During this session, Frederick could feel the release and freedom from hate in his body. As the tears flowed from his eyes, and a smile turned the corner of his lips, he could feel the warm energy of love filling him more deeply then he had ever felt it before.

This was a very exciting session for me to participate in. Here again is a wonderful example of how our soul decides upon a lesson to be learned during a physical incarnation. The assistance from other souls is elicited, we don our body-suits, and begin the drama, never remembering that we were the ones who called the players together.

This wonderful story shows how true forgiveness brings healing to us. It nourishes our soul and every cell of our physical being with love. It allows our energy to come home to us. This is why Jesus said, "Love your enemies." Until we can reach that place of love and forgiveness, it is our cells, body, mind, and spirit that suffer. If we want to feel loved and filled with the essence of God/Spirit then we must be willing to love and forgive ourselves as well as others.

Ann and Danny

Past-life contracts are often made at the time of death. The last feelings, thoughts, or words that we express carry over into our next lifetime. Contracts concerning relationships could be:

* I will never leave you again.
* I'll always take care of you.
* I'll get you back if it's the last thing I do!
* I will do anything you ask, just so you will never leave me.
* I will always love you.

These words and intentions may come from love, guilt, grief, or a combination of feelings. They tie the soul to the contract even in times where there is abuse. When a contract is in place, a normally logical person may act in illogical ways that are confusing to themselves and to others who know them. For example, a woman who may be genuinely loving and caring for her children may put up with the abuse of herself and them from a man who, "always promises to change." She may pack up and leave only to return to his apologies and a repeat pattern of abuse. Her friends may try to help, she may go to counseling to resolve father issues, early abuse issues, self-esteem issues, all the issues she can find, but the magnetic attraction to this one man remains.

Imagine a strong, outgoing man who does well in the business world, but in his personal life he allows himself to be manipulated and used by a woman whom he plans to marry. His friends may see this, try to talk to him about it, and even get angry with him. They may be confused as to why he will not listen to them or see for himself what is happening. He is the only one who feels the pull of the contract and, even though he does not know it on a conscious level, he is bound to his agreement. And so goes the story of Ann and Danny.

Ann and Danny were lovers. They had felt a strong connection at their first meeting five years ago at a college dance. Danny was handsome and well liked by his peers. There were many girls who would have loved to date him, but from the first moment they met he only "had eyes" for Ann. He was the perfect boyfriend: considerate, giving, true, and always there when Ann needed him-and she needed him a lot. Ann seemed to have no consideration for Danny. She flirted with other boys even when they were out together, and continued to do this even though she knew how it hurt him. She was demanding and belittled him often when they were out with friends. No one could understand what he saw in her. Well, maybe she was beautiful, but her attitude surely wasn't. None of Danny's friends liked her, they just put up with her for his sake. Danny always defended Ann and their relationship. He'd say things like, "That's the way she is, she doesn't mean any harm," or "It's different when we're alone together."

They became engaged. Danny began to have doubts and attempted to break off the engagement several times and each time was the same. Ann would cry and profess her love for Danny. She would make promises that she wouldn't keep, and she would always, somehow, make him feel guilty. He would end up apologizing for his behavior and bring her gifts to "make up." As their marriage date grew closer, Danny became more depressed until he seemed unable to make even simple decisions. This angered Ann and she threatened to leave. Although this break was what Danny knew was right and exactly what he needed, he could not bear the thought of losing her. Finally, he decided to seek help through hypnotherapy.

Danny drifted back in time, he found himself passing through the veil between lifetimes and entering a past life where, to his surprise, he was inhabiting the body of a woman. She was from a very wealthy family and had many suitors. One in particular was exceedingly fond of her and succeeded in winning her hand in marriage. Although this husband was very caring and good to her, she had affairs with other men and humiliated him in public. When Danny looked into the eyes of this husband, he recognized the eyes of Ann. As this lifetime progressed and Danny (then the wife) grew older, the husband (Ann), finally no longer able to withstand the abuse, called for a divorce and married a woman with whom he spent the rest of his life. The now divorced woman (Danny) lost her money and her beauty. She grew old alone and regretted having forced her husband away by her cruelty. She watched her ex-husband's reputation grow and saw that he was loved by many. At the time of death she said, "If I could only have him back I would do everything I could to make him happy."

Danny began to cry as he saw the contract he had made. The way Ann treated him probably had to do with anger that she carried over from that time. She may have possibly set up a contract of her own that claimed revenge on Danny for the humiliation she had suffered in that life. After Danny witnessed his death in the previous life and found the contract, I asked him to leave his body and go to the place where spirit dwells to find his soul lesson from that lifetime. His lesson was to value the heart above material wealth and social position. Danny had learned well. In his current life, although successful in the "real" world, his heart always came first.

I asked if he would like to go back and change anything in this past life. Danny said, "Yes," and went back to when he was born into that lifetime. With all the wealth his family had, he never received the love and appreciation that he desired. It was through this that he had learned to manipulate others and lose respect for material wealth. Danny imagined himself to be born into that family again, only this time he was loved and nurtured. He gained appreciation of himself and others. When he married, he honored the relationship because he now honored himself. When he followed this new life to its end, he and his partner were happy together and left that lifetime with a feeling of love for each other.

Can a past life experience be rewritten like a theater script? And, if it can, does this change the present? I believe that the answer to both questions is yes. Whether it be with inner child work or past life regression, our bodies, like computers, hold and are fundamentally affected by programmed memory. Memory is an energy that is stored in the cells. If this energy, or memory, is changed, the self seems to function in a different way. Changing the energy also causes a shift on the etheric plane which, in turn, affects others who are involved with the shift we make.

In the case of Danny and Ann, the energy shift led the couple to begin counseling. They postponed the wedding and made a commitment to work on their relationship. For the first time, Ann was willing to look at her behavior and understand that she needed counseling as well as Danny if they were to create a healthy relationship. Ann and Danny did marry two years later and continue their commitment to each other.

Ann and Danny were able to resolve their differences, respect each other, and commit to their relationship. However, there could have been a different ending. Danny could have released himself from the previous life's contract and Ann could have been furious with the energy shift. She could have tried harder to manipulate him and gain revenge. If this would have occurred, Danny, now free from guilt, would have been able to leave the relationship and move on with his life. There are many possibilities. The key is that once he made the shift, whatever followed would bring healthy resolution for him.

Soul Contracts

Ruth

Sometimes the soul connections and contracts that we make keep us in relationships that are illogical and dysfunctional. An example of this is the story of Ruth and Andrew.

Ruth had left her relationship with Andrew several times. Each time followed an episode where she was physically abused and made to feel stupid and worthless. Ruth would pack her bags and vow to not come back, but after only a few days her feelings of guilt would become so overwhelming that she would return, with apologies and promises to be a better wife.

This scenario repeated itself at regular intervals and even though Ruth received support from her family and friends to leave Andrew, she could not stay away from him. Finally, in desperation, she went to a therapist and became involved in a women's group. Although this gave her support and insight into her co-dependency issues, she was still unable to break away. When I first met Ruth she was experiencing great pain. She felt crazy. Her logical part told her to leave the relationship, but her seeming addiction to Andrew compelled her to stay.

We began a pastlife regression session that took Ruth to Victorian England. She was the daughter of a poor farmer and had experienced a difficult life. At about age eighteen she fell in love with a man who worked at a livery stable in a nearby village. Their courtship was passionate and there was a deep, heartfelt connection between them. They married, but times were difficult and their life was a financial struggle. Ruth was a beautiful woman with a bright, outgoing personality. A passing baron, about fifteen years her senior, noticed her one day. He wooed her secretly and in a short time promised to marry her and share his great wealth if she would consent to divorce her husband and marry him. Although this was difficult, both because of the times and because of the love she had for her husband, Ruth eventually gave in and became the baron's wife.

At first she enjoyed her fine clothes, jewels and home, but soon she became disenchanted with her new way of life. She had never loved the baron and continued to mourn for the relationship she had left. During one visit back home to see her ailing father, she heard news of her first husband. He had been so hurt by her rejection that he started to drink quite heavily and within the year had hung himself.

Ruth's sense of loss, grief, and guilt were overwhelming. Her heart became as cold as steel and she refused to allow love in. After the baron died she became a bitter and lonely widow whose wealth brought no happiness. At the time of her death in that lifetime she vowed that if she was ever again given the chance to be with this man whom she loved, she would endure all and never leave him. The man, of course, is Andrew. The illogical guilt that Ruth experienced came from her past-life guilt, which she took to her grave.

After her time of death in our session I asked Ruth if there was anything that she would like to change. She said Yes. She went back to the time when the baron asked her to marry him. She professed her love for her husband, made the decision to stay with him and rejected the baron's advances. They worked hard together, and succeeded in making a modest, but adequate living. They had two fine children and lived a contented and happy life. At her time of death in that changed lifetime, Ruth was surrounded by her children and grandchildren. Her husband had passed on the year before. She left her body in peace, looking forward to being united with him. With this change, the past-life contract was dissolved.

In this life, Andrew also had the unconscious past-life memory of being betrayed. Although he loved Ruth, his anger and hurt from that life ran over and contaminated his feelings for her in this life. The love he felt for Ruth, followed by his abuse of her, left Andrew feeling guilty and out of control. His way of dealing with the problem was to drink, the same method of coping he had used in that previous lifetime.

Ruth noticed an energetic shift after our session. She knew that, even though she loved Andrew, she could now take care of herself and leave the marriage for good. With her shift in energy an interesting thing happened with Andrew. He apparently felt the shift in Ruth and sensed that she was free, too. One night, a week after the session, Andrew uncharacteristically burst into tears and made the commitment to begin therapy. He had previously been unwilling to do so. Several years have passed now and Ruth and Andrew continue to learn and grow in their relationship. The abuse and drinking have stopped and they are living happily together.

When I teach hypnotherapy classes and work with clients, I always say that the reason to do this work is for your own understanding and healing, not to change someone else. A side benefit is that communication at this deep level often effects the other person as well. Unconsciously, we are connected to the energy of those around us. That connection is strongest with those who are closest to us. This is why Andrew felt the shift in Ruth. The fear that he felt at the possibility of losing her again compelled him to express his emotions and seek counseling. Because of Ruth's experience with hypnotherapy, Andrew also came to see me so that he could clear the energy he was holding from that lifetime.

Section IV
Personal Soul Contracts

Sometimes it seems to me that in this absurdly random life there is some inherent justice in the outcome of personal relationships. In the long run, we get no more than we have been willing to risk giving.

Sheldon Kopp

Recognizing Personal Soul Contracts

I have spoken about contracts that exist between souls for the purpose of healing and expanding conscious awareness. I would like now to talk about personal soul contracts, or contracts that we make with our own soul before we enter the physical plane. Such contracts are also made for the purpose of healing and awakening. We may call upon other souls to help us achieve our goal, but the main contract here is with the self.

Personal soul contracts can often be recognized in repeated patterns. If a person continually experiences a pattern of events, and that pattern persists though the players vary, there may be a belief which stems from present-life childhood trauma or past-life trauma where a personal soul contract exists. For example, if a woman finds herself being raped repeatedly, there may be a soul contract to learn about rape and forgive herself for times in a past life where she may have participated as a rapist. Or someone who frequently finds himself being fired, or always encountering a difficult boss, may have been the one in the past who treated employees or slaves unfairly. The person who always "falls in love" only to find the object of their attention leaving them for someone else may have carelessly broken hearts in another lifetime. Looking for what underlies such patterns is neither about justification nor blame. It is about gaining understanding and freedom.

The karmic wheel is ever turning. We may get away with "bad" behavior in one lifetime, but that behavior will follow us into our next incarnation. This is what it means in the biblical statement, "Do unto others as you would have them do unto you." The purpose of a personal soul contract is not for punishment, but for attaining higher awareness. When we experience all things, we find understanding, compassion, forgiveness, love of self, and love of others.

Past-life work has taught me about soul contracts. As we remember more of our past lives, we see that we have been it all (male, female, black, white, gay, straight, victim, persecutor), and done it all. When we realize this, there is less room to hate and to judge others, and less room to hate and judge ourselves. Through awareness and understanding of our contracts, we can stop repeating the old patterns and get off the karmic wheel.

When a pattern only occurs with one person, it is likely that a soul contract with that person is involved. Personal soul contracts, however, are a little different. They are not made with another being. They are made only with oneself. A personal soul contract may be present whenever you have been willing to work on healing an issue and no matter what you do, the issue still exists. You may have read, listened to tapes, done innerchild work, gone to seminars, tried traditional counseling or alternative therapies, and it still exists. Sure it may be better. You may have gained insights and healing, or noticed some other positive changes, but there, somewhere in your core you can still feel the pattern's pull. This is a classic sign of a personal soul contract.

If you notice yourself being continually attracted to studying a certain subject, doing a certain line of work, or working with a certain group of people, you may be experiencing the draw of a soul contract. Some of the most common issues that I have worked with concerning such contracts follow.

I teach hypnotherapy classes to people who are seeking to develop their healing skills. Ironically, I frequently find myself working with those who have made a personal soul contract to not do healing work. Well, you might ask, then why are they taking these classes? The answer is simple. Their souls have the desire and ability to work as healers, but they contracted in a past life to stay away from this work. The two most common reasons that I have found for such contracts are the abuse of power and persecution. Now their souls are being guided to release these contracts and move into self-healing and the awakening of their healing abilities. It appears that many healers who put the work aside in previous lives are now being called forth to assist on the planet at this time.

If a contract to stay away from healing work was made, it can be recognized by several behaviors. Among them are: the person continues to take classes but never feels ready to do the work; the person wants to take classes in healing but always has some excuse as to why they can't; or the person sets up a healing practice, but charges fees too low to support himself. These people often convince themselves and others that they have tried, thus gaining permission to retreat back into the safety of the "real" world. The story of Mary provides a perfect example of this.

Soul Contracts

Mary

Mary was a massage therapist who wanted to incorporate the use of herbs and flower remedies into her work. As soon as she started taking a class on the healing use of herbs she began to discount herself and her abilities. She became fearful of being able to do this work and was thinking about returning to her previous job as a legal secretary. Mary had always been a confident and independent person. She went after what she wanted and had been successful. These new fears were confusing and unfamiliar to her.

Because of Mary's past successes and self-confidence, I had the feeling that this current issue might be connected to a personal soul contract made in another lifetime. Mary wanted to explore this concept and we began a session with this in mind. In the session, Mary soon found herself living in a small cottage, in what appeared to be Seventeenth Century England. She was a wise woman and many people from a nearby village traveled to her home to receive the benefits of her work. Because she lived alone and rarely went into the town, the people were somewhat frightened of her. Mary did not seem to need anyone else. She grew, found, and dried her own herbs and flowers. She loved doing this and often spent days out in the forests and fields gathering her supplies. She was in contact with the devas who lived in her glen and regularly communicated with them.

It was a very peaceful life until a group of riders came into town talking about the devil and witchcraft. This frightened the villagers and they told the men about Mary. The men convinced the townsfolk that she was one of these witches and had been poisoning their souls. They led some of the people, carrying torches, to Mary's cottage. After shouting things like, "witch!" and "devil woman!" they set her home on fire. Terrified, Mary burned to her death. When Mary and I went back to that moment just before her death, Mary realized that she had made a contract to never do this work again.

During the next part of our session, I asked Mary if there was anything that she would like to change in that past life. She did not know what to do, so we asked her higher self to show her. She was brought back into that lifetime, only this time she did not do her work in secret. She made friends with the local pastor and two of the wealthiest and most respected families in the village. She educated them about the value of herbs and spoke of how they were gifts from God, and how He guided her to use them. She went into town weekly, attending service at the local church and became well liked by the townspeople. This time, when the men rode into town the people did not even think of Mary when the men spoke of the evil of witches. There was no energy in this town for these men so they rode on their way.

Mary next went to that place where spirit lives and asked what the learning was for her from that time. She was told that the lesson was to awaken to the importance of including others. Instead of "doing" things to people it was time for her to educate them and be an assistant in their healing process. The energy change that occurred in reliving the past life allowed Mary to relax and enjoy her present-day study of herbal and flower remedies.

From this session, it is easy to understand how Mary could be successful when pursuing a variety of healing modalities, but became frightened as soon as she began exploring herbal remedies. Her soul had drawn her to the herbal remedy class as a way of waking her up to receive the lesson she needed and do the work in which she was skilled. Instead of meeting the fear, Mary could have given in to it and returned to her old job where she probably would have never felt fulfilled and, perhaps, may have even become ill or depressed.

Soul Contracts

The Money Contract

Money is another key area in which personal contracts create patterns. I have worked with many people who have abused power and material wealth in the past and have made contracts not to allow this to happen again. Sometimes these people are born into the belief system that money is dirty, bad, unholy, or corrupt. This is a great protective system because it allows the individual to forego the desire for material wealth for virtuous and holy reasons. This works until the individuals decide, one day, that they might want to have a greater abundance in their life. They may decide that it's time to get out of the low income bracket and travel, have a nice home, pretty things, fine clothes, or other things that money can buy. At this point, a little voice inside comes out with something like: "How selfish. You should be happy with what you have....look at the poverty in Russia, China, Africa, etc. You should be ashamed."

A frequent next step is to buy books on creating prosperity, or to take classes or engage in therapy. Through such means we can examine all our issues around self-worth and deserving. We may come to the place of saying, "Yes, I am worthy. I do deserve abundance." But, then the money doesn't come, or it comes into our lives only to be stopped by some unforeseen event of self-sabotage. The feeling of hopelessness usually follows, and we think, "No r what I do, nothing seems to work." If you find this or a similar scenario in your life, it might be a good time to check and see if you may have made a past life contract regarding wealth. If there is a hidden fear that having wealth will lead to abuse of power, that fear will kick in and take over as soon as money begins to accumulate.

Let's take the story of George. George was born into a middle-class family and was always told what a good boy he was because he rarely asked his parents for anything. He always seemed happy with whatever he had and this pleased his parents. When his siblings persisted in making demands of their parents to buy them things, his mother would always say, "Why can't you be like your brother, he never asks for anything." So George grew up and became attached to this "virtue." George thought of himself as pious and was glad that he did not succumb to the "ways of the world." This made him feel as if he were better than his brothers, sisters, and everyone else who concerned themselves with material goods. Life went on this way until George was thirty-two and his soul decided that it was time for him to become conscious. His wake up call came through a young woman named Margaret.

Margaret was pretty, bright, and talented. She appreciated George's simple life until they seriously began to consider the possibility of marriage. Although Margaret valued the balance George brought into her life, he didn't reciprocate. He began criticizing her about how she spent her money. This created a friction in their relationship and Margaret decided that although his simple way of living was endearing, she wanted to have nice things, travel, and provide well for any children she might have. Margaret was ready to break off the engagement when George came to see me in hope that hypnotherapy might help him to save his relationship.

Our first step was to do inner-child work, enabling George to recognize his talents and strengths while letting go of his attachment to "virtuous" poverty. After our second session, we decided that it might be helpful to see if there was a past life connection to George's issue of pious poverty.

In this next session, George found himself in Egypt. He was an aide to the king and took delight in bedecking himself with fine clothes, gold and jewels. His responsibility, it seemed, was to oversee a large group of slaves who were constructing a building for the king. Each day George would ride out in a wagon-type vehicle, which he described as having two large wheels and being pulled by a team of horses. It was very hot and the slaves worked very hard. George was proud of how they stopped their work to bow when he came by. He wanted them to admire his elegant wardrobe and know that he was favored by the king. He had no compassion for the slaves and spoke harshly to the captains. He took pleasure in watching the slaves beaten and shown their place.

I had George go through this lifetime, learning whatever was important for him to know. He came to a scene where he had wandered far out into the fields alone. He felt himself fall as his foot sunk into a hole and his ankle turned. There was great pain and he could not get up. At that moment, a small group of slaves came into view, carrying a heavy stone. George waved his arm and demanded that they come and pick him up. He saw the slaves carry the stone toward him, then felt the crushing sensation as they dropped it over his body. Going back to that incident just before death, George felt his own terror, but he also noticed the faces of those men with the stone. For the first time he felt *their* pain. For an instant he regretted his actions and made the contract to never abuse wealth and power in that way again.

George did not want to go back and change the story. What he needed was to meet with this past-life part of himself and do forgiveness work. As George held this part, cried, and forgave himself, I did energy work over his body. I prayed that the cells be released of the pain, yet keep the knowledge and compassion that they gained from the past life. This was quite a difficult session for George and two weeks later he was still processing all that had happened.

George noticed a shift in his life after this last session. He found that he was kinder to himself and that his relationship with Margaret was better. He shared the story of his session with Margaret, who was open to his experience. Today they are communicating much better in their relationship, and George has even purchased the occasional special gift for Margaret.

Through self-forgiveness George was able to release his contract from the past life and understand that he can be materially abundant and at the same time be compassionate and loving. To reinforce this understanding, George chooses to donate money and carpentry skills to a shelter for the homeless. He now sees money as an energy that can be used to both care for himself and help others.

Money issues are commonly rooted in personal soul contracts. I see this revealed again and again with clients and students.

John and
the AIDS Virus

I also see soul contracts played out through illness. The following story of a man whom I will call John is a profound example of this.

John had developed *kaposi's sarcoma*, a cancer of the skin which can occur in people with AIDS. John's holistic doctor had suggested hypnotherapy as a therapeutic option, and so John sought me out. After explaining the process of Spiritual Hypnosis to John, he decided that he wanted to explore any message the AIDS virus had for him.

To begin our session, I took John into a medium trance state. John soon found himself riding a horse into a castle courtyard. The scene was clearly that of Europe in the Middle Ages. As he approached the heavy stone walls he felt the excitement of returning home after being away at war. The massive wooden gates were open, as if in anticipation of his return. As he rode into the center of the courtyard he noticed a young woman with a baby in her arms running out to meet him. She was his wife and the child was their daughter. He reached down and picked up the little girl, and as he did so his wife exclaimed, "Everyone has the plague here, even our daughter!" Upon hearing these words, John threw the baby back into his wife's arms, turned his horse around and galloped away from that place. He rode and rode until he was exhausted. Both he and his horse needed rest and water. Finding a small pond, he stopped and got down from his horse. As he bent down over the water, John saw the mark of the plague reflected back in his own face. In fear and despair, he took up his sword and plunged it through his heart.

One of the most powerful moments of pastlife regression work comes when the person recalls the time of death. At the time of death, we often make our soul contracts for the next lifetime. I asked John to go back to the time just before he plunged the sword into his heart and notice what his last words or thoughts were. What came to him was, "I will come back for another plague and this time I won't run!"

John did come back for another plague, AIDS, and this time he didn't run. He contracted the HIV virus very early on and, instead of taking the recommended drug called AZT, he focused on natural healing resources. He talked to his friends about natural choices and watched as, one-by-one they took AZT, got sicker and sicker and then died from this plague.

John's Spiritual Hypnosis session was just one piece of his healing program. Through our session, he became conscious of his soul's contract and the reason why he made this contract. Because of his commitment to healing and his positive outlook on life, John is healthy and living a happy and productive life these many years later. He no longer associates himself with having AIDS.

Judy

Soul contracts provide us with profound lessons. When we become conscious of these contracts and the events leading to them, we gain great insight and are able to break the patterns that bind us to the past. We become free to move forward. Other people are always part of our growth. Sometimes our souls gather in family clusters that support individual soul contracts. This was the case for Judy.

Judy, a close friend of mine, had been keeping a secret for many years. Finally she was willing to share this secret and to feel the shame she connected with it. Many years ago, when Judy was a young woman and the mother of four children, she had gotten involved in an abusive relationship. Her two youngest children were born from that relationship. When Judy decided to leave the relationship, her husband threatened to kill her and all of the children. Judy bravely took the children and moved into a friend's house despite these threats. But since the husband knew where Judy worked, she never felt safe and was always afraid that he would find them. This was a terrifying time for her.

Judy remained in contact with her husband's sister who relayed messages between them. One such message from him was that if Judy let his sister adopt his two children he would leave her and her other two children alone. His sister, who wanted to have children but could not have them naturally, was happy to agree to this arrangement. Judy liked the sister and felt that this woman could offer the children a more stable and secure life than she could provide at the time, so she agreed to the adoption. Even though she felt this was the best thing for the children, the decision was very difficult and brought her much pain and shame. Her son, Jack Jr., was four and her daughter, Gail, was three at the time. Judy cried as she shared this story and related how little Jack had clung to her crying, "Take me home mommy!"

Judy had carried this pain within her heart for nearly twenty-five years. She felt great shame for not being able to better care for these children whom she dearly loved, and even greater shame for giving them up.

Judy and I had become friends through our study of Alchemical Hypnotherapy. We have both been committed to doing our work, and today Judy is the owner of the school for which I teach. She asked that I use her real name because she says that she kept this secret long enough, and now, through her prayers and this work, healing has come. I feel honored to share her story in these pages. The story is a rich example of how beings come together to complete individual personal soul contracts. Judy's contract and that of her children, was revealed in our session together.

About two years ago, Judy began to search for her children. She paid an agency a finder's fee and waited. She wanted to know how they were and begin some communication with them, if they were willing. She waited for several months and had only received one envelope containing nothing she found useful. One day, during a hypnotherapy class that she was teaching, the students broke up into practice groups and by "coincidence" it turned out that Judy had the opportunity to teach a co-induction (where two people use their voices simultaneously to induce trance) piece with herself as the subject. They asked if there was anything special that she wanted to work on and she said, "No". Then, all of a sudden the tears came, and for the first time she shared her story. During the session, an inner guide told her that she must do another session about this before being reunited with her children, and the guide suggested that she do the session with me.

Judy lived in Spokane and a few months following that session with her students I flew out to her school to teach a hypnotherapy class. I always left for home as soon as class was finished, but this time I decided to stay one extra night so that Judy and I would have time for a session exchange. This occurred a few months after Judy's guide had suggested that she receive a session from me, and at that time I was unaware of this suggestion.

When the time came for Judy's session, she told me the story of her children. She asked that the focus of her session be on finding them. As she she went into the trance state, Judy entered into a past-life story in which she and a man were walking across a desert. He had no covering for his feet and Judy never offered to share what she had with him. The man's feet were badly blistered and he was in great pain when they finally walked into a town. The townsfolk pitied the man and took care of him while they chastised Judy for her lack of compassion. In watching this scenario, Judy felt waves of sadness and shame move through her body. Her guide told her that this was one of many lifetimes in which she had been shamed and that her soul contract for this lifetime was to release the shame. Her guide went on to say that she and her two youngest children had made an agreement to assist each other in healing deep issues in this lifetime. Both children carried issues of abandonment into this lifetime. I can just imagine these three souls talking before coming down into the physical plane. "I want to heal this shame I've been carrying around for lifetimes." "We want to heal this abandonment issue. Hey, I have an idea! Why don't you be our mom? Then you can leave us so we can really feel the abandonment and you can feel the shame." "Deal?" "Deal." And so, the contract was made. Each soul had its personal contract and commitment to healing, as well as an agreement to assist the others in their individual contracts.

After learning of the contract agreements, Judy saw a bird's nest full of baby birds, their necks stretched out and beaks open. Immediately she noticed how drained she felt, always giving to her children, grandchildren, husband, students, etc. She said, "Everybody always wants something from me!" As she got closer to the birds she was shocked to hear that what they were really crying was, "Leave us alone!"

In that moment, Judy saw how the shame she had been holding was driving her to "do everything and be everything" for everyone. It was this force, rather than outside circumstances, that compelled her to take care of others. She imagined letting the birds take care of themselves and watched how even a fall from the nest created an opportunity for growth, an opportunity that they wouldn't have had if she had stepped in to help.

Judy now understood that the drama she lived in this life was agreed upon before incarnation, and that the experience provided the opportunity for powerful healing for everyone concerned. Judy was able to communicate with the souls of Gail and Jack. She shared elings of love for them and felt that love returned. as then able to release the shame which had taken up a large portion of the center of her body, all the way from her heart to her power center, just above the navel. In its place she brought in the piece of herself that had left to make room for the shame. This piece had to do with self-love. As self-love filled the space where shame once lived, Judy felt a deep sense of peace and love for herself and for her children. This was a very sacred moment of deep spiritual, emotional, and cellular healing. This healing unfolded in her life in a beautiful way.

Judy had been upset with the agency she had hired to locate her children. She felt that they had only given her information which she could have accessed herself on the internet. She was going to stop payment to them because they hadn't provided the promised service. About a week after our session, Judy was searching for her agency account number in order to cancel their services when she discovered a paper she had not seen before. On this paper was the phone number of a contact person for her daughter. Even though she had looked through the information in the envelope when it arrived several months earlier, she had never seen this piece. Spirit works in marvelous ways.

Judy immediately called the contact number on the paper and was soon speaking with her daughter. They had a joyful, tearful reunion over the phone. Judy learned that her daughter had been searching for her for about five years, but had finally given up after using a Ouija board. The letters of the Ouija board had spelled out, "Stop looking. She will find you."(The Ouija board is only a tool that, when used with right intention, allows our subconscious, Higher Self, and Spirit to communicate with us.)

As I write this, Judy is preparing for a family re-union. Gail, Gail's husband, and a grandson whom Judy has never met will be coming "home." Gail will be reunited with her mom and two sisters and will meet a new dad, brothers-in-law and several nephews. Judy has now also spoken with her son, Jack, and his wife, and they are looking forward to the time when they will be together. Though there was great pain in the past, Judy's Gail's and Jack's honesty and willingness to communicate has brought great healing to the present.

My Personal Journey

I love the way Carolyn Myss talks about how we make our soul plan and then descend onto the physical plane with our angel hollering out after us, "But you're not going to remember any of this!" Being such a visual person, that image makes me smile as my heart resonates with its truth. By becoming conscious of and understanding our soul contracts, we can find the lessons that our soul agreed to learn and release the thoughts of anger, blame, betrayal, guilt and shame that we hold towards ourselves and others. We can find forgiveness, peace, and love.

Though we may find great pain connected with past-life contracts, the reason for those contracts is not to make us suffer. If we are to become powerful, abundant beings, embracing ourselves and all of our talents, we need to learn how to live compassionately. Our lessons show us many aspects of ourselves and of humanity. Our willingness to do this work allows us to become whole beings who truly live from our heart center.

In doing this work I have naturally been curious to explore my personal soul contracts. Several years ago, I received a hypnotherapy session which took me back to the time of my conception in 1948. I experienced my spirit as an expanded energy which immediately felt crushed upon entering my mother's womb. There was a feeling of panic as I thought, "I don't want to be here! I want to get out!" This was followed by the violent sensation that I was being crushed. This sensation was so intense that my body began to contort and I could "see" large sandstone boulders rolling upon me and crushing me to death. As I further regressed, I witnessed an avalanche covering my body. In that moment, I realized that this feeling of being crushed was brought into my present-day body. This time, however, the crushing experience was emotional and spiritual rather than physical.

My soul made a contract to learn lessons that would give me the courage and strength to stand in my power and integrity without fear or shame. In the moment of this revelation my whole life made sense. The pieces fell together and I understood how everything and everyone in my life, no matter how painful or difficult, was there to support me in attaining this goal.

As the session continued, I settled down and began to feel the excitement of moving through the birth canal. This enthusiasm quickly transformed into a deep sense of shame as my genitals emerged. Oh no! I was supposed to have been a boy! This began a series of life experiences that reinforced the shame and belief that I was not good enough now, nor could I ever be. I was shamed for being overly sensitive, for not doing the right things or acting the right way. At nineteen I became anorexic. It was in 1968, I was in nursing school, and eating disorders had not yet entered the public eye. Twiggy was in and a girl couldn't be too thin. No one noticed that I was starving myself to death. As I look back, I see that it was the shame, lack of self-love and ke it was wrong to want to live my own life that ; acted out through this self abuse.

Often I hear clients say, "I only want to understand why this happened to me. Why was I treated this way? Why did my parents abuse me? What did I do to deserve this? Why was I abandoned?" Personally, I don't believe that there is any excuse or reason for abuse from the physical dimension point of view. Looking for the why in this dimension usually fails us. You may come to realize that abusers abused us because they were abused, but that offers little solace. Seeking the answer in this dimension can keep you looking for someone or something to blame and keep you from healing. Focusing on the why keeps you from opening to the lesson, reclaiming your personal power, and living your life in a full and healthy way.

Letting go and seeking the big picture may not be an easy task. The key for me has been to take the question beyond this physical world and into the soul's dimension. What did your soul choose to come into this life-time to learn? How do the events and people in your life contribute to your soul plan? Often it seems that we receive the opposite of what we wanted. For example the soul who came to learn self-love may be abandoned, the soul who came to learn non-judgement may be discriminated against, and the soul who came to learn compassion may find anguish. For myself, it was feeling like I didn't fit in, that I wasn't good enough, and that I couldn't do or say the right thing that gave me the insight, compassion and strength to be who I am today. Without these experiences and the people in my life, I would not have had the opportunities I needed to grow, heal and learn what was important for me. Today, I love who I am, I love my life, and I am thankful for every situation and every person who assisted me in becoming who I am today.

I certainly didn't always feel this way. I was angry and blamed others for my pain and for their treating me unjustly. I have been praying and asking God and my guides for many years to help me to see the big picture. I believe that whenever we sincerely ask Spirit for help, that help is given to us. Here is one story from my life that reminds me of this.

One day, I was going through a particularly rough time with a foster child who was using crystal meth (a man-made chemical substance which is extremely destructive to both body and mind). I knew that I had become so enmeshed in his web of drugs and lies that I was losing control of my own life. I didn't know what to do. I went into Seattle to visit with a friend and all the way home that night I prayed for a message that could help me. I drove into our driveway, parked my car in the garage, and as I walked up the stairs to our front door I found a hawk. He was lying on his back with his wings folded over his abdomen as if he were in prayer. He was dead. As I looked at him I felt as if he had been placed there for me, perfectly parallel with the door and every feather in place. Emotion flooded through my body as I walked inside and straight to my medicine cards. I read how Hawk flies high near Grandfather Sun and sees across the valleys. The message was very clear to me. I was stuck in a valley and not looking at the whole picture. I was caught up in trying to rescue my foster son from what I perceived to be destructive behavior without taking into account that he might be doing exactly what he needed for his soul's growth. With a deep breath, I breathed in peace with this reminder that God, not I, was in charge. Sometimes we want things to be different for ourselves or for others. When we live in the valley and look for change on the valley floor we continue to move in limited ways. But when we fly, like

Hawk, up near Grandfather Sun, we become aware of the big picture and of our unlimited possibilities. With this perspective comes greater understanding, less judgement, and the freedom to live our lives in ways that bring us healing, love, and joy. Each day I pray to be as close as I can be to Spirit. Each day I face the challenges presented to me and I look, as best as I am able, to see them from the soul's perspective. The more I trust that everything is for my good, the more I find myself finding the gifts each situation brings. As I do this, my life continues to grow more positive, peaceful, and powerful.

Just last week, a concert by the Seattle Lesbian and Gay Chorus brought another opportunity for me to look from the soul's perspective. In the first half of the program, concert members, through music and spoken word, told the story of Bobby. Bobby was a twenty-year-old gay man who committed suicide because being gay was unacceptable to his family and to his church. He and his mother had prayed for several years for God to change him. Finally, unable to deal any longer with the pain, and feeling like he must be completely unworthy for God not to answer his prayers, Bobby jumped from a freeway bridge into the path of a semi-truck. He died instantly.

Bobby's grief-stricken mother read about her son's suffering in the journal that Bobby left behind. She began to question the teachings of her church and reached out to other religious institutions to find what they were saying about being gay. In her search, she found many churches of all denominations who were open and affirming to gays and lesbians. She realized that it was her minister, and not God, who was saying that it was wrong to be gay. This mother finally found the answer to why God wouldn't help her son. That answer was: God had made him perfectly and he didn't need changing.

Bobby's mother now works with young gay and lesbian people and their families because she never wants anyone to have to go through the pain that her family experienced.

I was deeply touched when I heard how Bobby, in spirit form, visits his mother and tells her that he is proud of what she is doing. Bobby has also told his mother that he is happy where he is. There was probably not one dry eye in the audience, including mine, by the end of this story. But, rather than looking at this as only a tragedy and seeing Bobby as a victim of religious persecution, I felt that this young man and his mother had a powerful soul contract.

From my perspective, both the connection Bobby's mother had with this particular church and the love she has for her son enables her to speak out in a powerful way. There is no one better to address religious beliefs that spawn hate for gays and lesbians than this woman. Bobby has brought the gift of his struggle and story into the world at a time when gays and lesbians are seeking to be included in society with the same opportunities for housing, jobs, marriage, and families straight people have.

There is no justification, on this physical plane, for the torment that Bobby was forced to endure. But on the spiritual plane, in the light of soul contracts, this young man's life was lived for a purpose. This story is a potent example of how important it is for each one of us to seek the truth and not blindly believe what we are told, even when we are told by someone who has authority or is supposed to be an expert. Love is the answer, and any action based in fear and hate is diametrically opposed to love, to the truth, and to God.

Section V

A Spiritual Approach to Abortion

We're swimming through a river of change. We've spent the last decade standing on the river bank, rescuing women who are drowning. In the next decade, some of us have to go to the head of the river to keep women from falling in.

Gloria Steinam

About the Process

For some years now I have been providing special sessions to women who find themselves pregnant when they do not wish to be. I call these sessions a "spiritual approach to abortion." I believe that we are spirit and that we have come into the physical realm for learning and experience. If this is so, then why not communicate with the spirit of the unborn child and let it know that this is not right timing?

This approach enables the unborn child to consciously participate in the abortion decision. It is a loving approach that seems to be tremendously healing. The basis for the spiritual abortion process comes from the belief that when you enter the physical realm as a baby, your body is small and needs to be taken care of, but your soul may be old and full of wisdom. If this is true for a baby then it is also true for the unborn child, the one just beginning to develop a physical body inside of the womb that carries it. We can communicate with this spirit just as we can with a loved one who has passed on. The spirit of an unborn child is filled with wisdom and always has a powerful lesson to share with the mother and father.

In 1991, I wrote an article entitled the "Spiritual Approach to Abortion" for the Seattle New Times, a metaphysical newspaper. I received numerous letters and telephone calls from women who read this article.

Many women wanted to tell me their story of "spontaneous" abortion, how they had prayed, meditated, lit candles, chanted and than naturally miscarried. As I heard and read these accounts a part of me awakened to the knowledge that this process was natural for women in times long past. There was a time, I believe, when women understood the power and the sacredness of their bodies and made conscious choices about when to give, or not give birth. This ability is awakening in us now. We are longing for and looking to return to this ancient wisdom of the Goddess.

Spiritual Hypnotherapy makes it possible for the mother to connect with the spirit of the child, and for them to agree upon a natural miscarriage. Of the women I have worked with, several have naturally miscarried shortly after their sessions while others have needed to have clinical abortions. When women have clinical abortions scheduled just following their session and they follow through with the abortion, it is impossible to know whether or not the process would have occurred naturally. My belief is that as more women become aware of this option, it will become easier for them to have natural abortions, and that it will become easier for women to consciously choose when to become pregnant.

Women from all over the country have called me to ask who in their area is doing spiritual abortion work. I was not aware of others doing this work so I would explain the process over the telephone and wish them well. After having received several return calls from these women, and finding that some were able to naturally miscarry, I decided to make an audio tape. The tape is for those wishing to abort as well as for those who wish to heal from past abortion or miscarriage.

One Christian woman who had become pregnant, but who was not ready to have a child requested the tape because her religion does not permit abortion. She and her boyfriend said that they would listen to it and leave the results to God. The woman called me two weeks later with the news that after she and her boyfriend listened to the tape several times, she miscarried. For more information on this tape, please see the appendix at the end of this book.

From a practical standpoint, as anyone in the business world knows, responsibility must accompany authority in order for a system to be effective. Although women hold the responsibility for childbearing, in many cultures it has been the men who take the power or assume authority. We don't have to look far back into history before we see such prevailing views as "barefoot and pregnant," and "A woman's place is in the home." Even popular songs from the sixties encourage young girls to "Wear your hair just for him." Generally speaking, men took, and still take pride in getting their wives pregnant, especially when a son is involved. Still in some cultures today, the more children, especially male children, a man fathers, the more manly or favored he is thought to be. Women often had to take responsibility for their pregnancies through birth control, but even birth control was or is not allowed by certain major religions. I wonder if, because men cannot bear children themselves, they felt inadequate or fearful of a woman's power and historically have striven to make it appear as if they are in control. I want to stress here that I , in no way, include all men in this statement. There are many, many men who honor and support women's rights. And men do share the responsibilities entailed in childbearing.

Spiritual Hypnotherapy is extremely valuable for both actual abortion and healing from miscarriage. It is valuable for both women and men. Although the mother carries the child, there is learning for the father as well. Sometimes the spirit of the fetus is even more connected to the father than to the mother. When an abortion or miscarriage takes place and there is usually no spiritual healing involved, feelings such as grief, guilt, anger, and fear may become stuck in the body. In a woman, these often center in the reproductive organs. Naturopathic physicians have told me that most women who have ovarian cancer, cysts, fibroid tumors, abnormal bleeding, and other "female problems" have experienced an abortion or miscarriage. In our modern medical environment, a hysterectomy is often offered as the "cure."

The womb is the center of the feminine body. It is the birthing center of creativity, but the beauty of this is little recognized in our society. In this country, women commonly hear, "You're not going to have any more children," or, "You're past the childbearing age," "so let's do a hysterectomy." What message does this give to a woman? I think that the message that a woman receives is that her creative worth is defined by bearing children. I bring attention to this because claiming personal power and creativity has been the major issue with several of my clients. Pregnancy fills the womb. The baby becomes the creation and the pay-off is safety. Society claims it acceptable for a woman to focus on birth and babies. Childbearing can be a good camouflage for those who are afraid to look into themselves and face the fears, doubts, and inadequacies that keep their expression of personal creative force at a distance. Of course, these women are not aware that they are masking something until they take that journey within the self.

Men also hold unresolved feelings in their bodies. With respect to childbearing issues, I'm not certain where in the body men hold this energy. Men who have been partners in abortion/miscarriage have suggested to me that this energy may concentrate in the third chakra, which is the center of power. In the case of miscarriage, a man might feel that he was not powerful, potent, or "manly" enough to save the baby. In abortion, it might be that the man feels that he did something wrong, that it was his fault and he doesn't deserve to have what he wants. I'm sure that there are many other possible beliefs or feelings. If you are a man who has had an experience with miscarriage or abortion, take a moment to close your eyes and imagine the experience, feel your feelings around this issue and notice where they live in your body.

Spiritual Hypnosis allows the woman to go deep within the womb to explore core beliefs and judgements held by her as well as by women throughout the fabric of time, past and present. Some common beliefs are that women: need to nurture others and not put themselves first; must have children to be worthwhile; need a man to take care of them; are the "weaker sex"; and are not in control of their bodies. Many women who perceive themselves to be independent, strong, and free-thinking have been appalled to find such beliefs lurking in their innermost psyche. It is amazing to see how core beliefs which we are consciously unaware of, or thought we had let go of, determine what we attract into our lives. Through the Spiritual Hypnotherapy process, these hidden elements come to the surface where they can be healed and released.

With every "spiritual abortion" session, the child's spirit brings a message of learning to the mother and father. In many instances, this message involves the importance of nurturing and caring for one's own inner child. Women who are questioning whether or not to have a child can contact and support the child within. This liberates them from the "need" to have a child so that they are free to make a healthy choice about pregnancy.

I believe that it would be good for every person who wants a child to do inner-child work prior to conception. One of the most common issues between parents and children is the desire of the parent to control the child and mold the child into what the parent wants. When the child, desiring to find a healthy, independent identity rebels, the pain and separation that results is often blamed on the child. To avoid this, the child may instead become the "good" child and live his or her life trying to please the parent rather then fully becoming his/her own person. If a parent is not nurturing his/her own inner child, the outer child becomes a substitute and focal point for the parent. Thus, in place of a functional, supportive parent who encourages the child to individuate, we find the dysfunctional parent who controls, either subtly or overtly, to have their own needs fulfilled by the child.

When a woman chooses to do a spiritual abortion session prior to having a clinical abortion, she is often able to learn the lesson from the pregnancy as well as speak directly to the spirit of the child. Some of the most common lessons the spirit comes to teach are about healing the inner child, bringing forth creative energy, empowering the self, healing relationship issues, and healing from past abortions or miscarriages so that the mother may choose a healthy new pregnancy. Sometimes the connection between the woman and the unborn child runs very deep and the mother can experience feelings of great love and pain in letting go. It is important to remember that pain does not equal bad or wrong. A right choice in our lives can bring feelings of loss, grief, or loneliness and still be the right choice for us. For example, leaving an abusive relationship can bring up many painful feelings and still be the best, healthy choice for us.

Spirit is so loving that I have had many clients burst into tears when they feel this energy because it is the purest love they have ever felt. There is no demand, no desire, no judgement. There is only love. Over and over I have been witness to how loving and forgiving Spirit can be.

One concern that has been expressed to me is the fear that anytime we take action to keep a spirit from taking on a physical body, we deny life and that is wrong. In my experience, there are times when the spirit wants or has contracted, to communicate and is willing to take on a physical body in order to do this, but does not prefer it this way. By its very nature, spirit is alive, so we cannot deny a spirit life. To think that our physical plane is desired by all and is the ultimate experience may be a bit presumptuous. Through the work that I have done, I have felt and seen how loving and forgiving Spirit is, how connected the physical and spiritual world are, and how important it is for each one of us to honor our highest truth.

I have been asked if there are times when a spirit does not agree to leave and the answer is yes, this does happen. But the only times I have experienced this were with women who had issues of not taking their own power and always wanting to please others. I remember three cases like this when the spirit came forth with, "No, I will not go." Each time the client had to work on being willing to make the right choice for herself. Each time when this point of power came, the spirit was joyful and expressed that this was the lesson to be learned.

Just because spirit is Spirit does not mean that it is experiencing an "enlightened" state of being. When a spirit has been aborted without prior communication, it may remain around the mother's energy field in a confused, frightened, or angry state. This occurred for one of my clients who became pregnant and "just had a feeling like something was wrong." She shared with me that she had an abortion three years earlier and was worried that this might affect the child she was now carrying. When she entered into a deep state of being during the session, she suddenly became afraid. She said,"There's something out here and I'm afraid it's going to hurt my child!" I could feel the energy in my body as well, and I could feel her fear. When I asked if she knew who it was, she immediately got that it was the spirit of the child she had aborted. It was a male energy and he was very angry that this little girl child was in the womb. He said, "I was supposed to be the one!" The client became even more fearful when she heard this. I asked if there were any guides that could come to care for this one. Immediately angels came and began to surround him with love. His energy softened, and as he began to move away with them he also began to forget her. The client saw that he would be born to someone else and would enter into this world again in a healthier state of being. She felt at peace with her decision of abortion and was able to carry on with her pregnancy with a positive energy.

When I speak of Spiritual Abortion, some people become concerned that helping women to awaken to this process will encourage people to be reckless with preventing pregnancy because they can "just talk to the spirit and tell it to go. "I do not think that such recklessness is likely. Doing this work takes commitment to self-healing. It is an inner process that requires courage and the willingness to explore individual truth. It is a spiritual process and not a simple command ordering a spirit to leave. This work does not encourage abortion, but allows for the spiritual healing of mother, father, and child when abortion is the choice. I truly believe that as women become more aware of Spirit and inner healing work, they will communicate more easily with their bodies and themselves as a whole, and this will result in fewer unwanted pregnancies.

I have spoken mainly of the mother with regard to this work because it is she who generally comes to do these sessions. But I have worked with both parents together, and I have worked solely with the father. At these times, I have witnessed men do wonderful healing work by communicating with the child they had lost, or were soon to lose through miscarriage or abortion. One of the lessons that frequently comes up for men is fear of commitment. A spirit child once told her grieving father, "When you can clearly commit to fathering a child you shall have one." Other lessons that come up for men are those of the wounded inner child and relationship issues.

I have selected the following stories to illustrate this Spiritual Approach to Abortion process. I hope that these stories will give you greater insight as to how Spirit can make itself known through pregnancy, and how a spirit may contract to assist a woman, or man, in achieving greater consciousness and healing.

Soul Contracts

Andrea

Andrea was a very pretty young woman who came to me because she wasn't sure if she wanted the child she was carrying. She was considering a medical abortion. She and the father had been together for nearly two years and he was looking forward to beginning a family. They were planning to marry someday and the pregnancy ushered that day forward. Andrea told me that she and the father had a very good relationship and that she felt he would make an excellent father. The problem was her. She felt that she didn't deserve to have a child and that she would be inadequate as a mother.

As we spoke, Andrea confided that she had already had two abortions, one at age sixteen and another at nineteen. As a result, she was afraid that this baby would not be born healthy. She was afraid that her body had been damaged and that she would be "punished" for having had the abortions. I told Andrea about how other women had connected with the spirits of those who were aborted or miscarried and asked her if she would be willing to try to access these souls. She said that she was afraid, but that she would like very much to contact these beings.

Both of the spirits were female in energy. They came to Andrea quickly and she felt their presence as well as their love. They told her that they loved her and forgave her but that she needed to forgive herself. Andrea cried and said that she did not know how to do this, nor even if she could. I had her call forth her sixteen-year-old self. She, this Andrea, was shy and scared. I asked the present Andrea to look into the eyes of the sixteen-year-old Andrea. At first she didn't want to, she only felt anger for this young girl. Then finally she was able to connect with this self and feel her pain. She began to understand how this young girl was only looking for love and, coming from an abusive home, was willing to look anywhere. A young man had spoken the words she longed to hear, "I love you," but left her as soon as she told him that she was pregnant. Andrea was left with feelings of shame and guilt. She felt that her only choice was to have an abortion. Although her parents supported this decision, they made certain that she knew that they disapproved of her actions. Andrea wept as she remembered her pain and finally was able to hold her sixteen-year-old self and tell her that she loved her and that she forgave her.

Meeting herself at nineteen was easier for Andrea because she had already done the first healing. The situations were similar, and Andrea forgave this young woman as well. As all three Andreas embraced and held hands, the present-day Andrea felt a freedom and inner love that she had not known before. The spirits of her unborn children told Andrea that they had been waiting for her to recognize them so that she could receive their love and, most importantly, forgive herself. They said that this new baby was also a girl and that Andrea would make a fine mother, but that it was very important for her to forgive herself first. They told her that the spirit of this baby would feel the energy shift with this forgiveness and self love. This would energetically shift the baby's consciousness as well and she would be happier for it. Andrea felt a great sense of relief, self forgiveness, and self love. She felt her desire to have this child.

Today she is a happy mother who loves her little daughter very much.

In this story, we see how there was a contract with the spirits of the first two pregnancies. They agreed to stay with Andrea until the time she was able to speak with them and learn this lesson of self-love and forgiveness. After this was completed, the spirits were free to move into the light of the spirit realm.

Soul Contracts

Molly

Molly had married and raised three children. At the age of forty she was pregnant again, but neither she or her husband wanted another child. They were using birth control and felt somewhat betrayed to find themselves in this situation. Although Molly logically agreed that it was not in their family's best interest to have another child, she also felt a relief in being pregnant. Her youngest son was eighteen and would be leaving home for college in the fall. In the past, Molly had somehow always ensured that at least one of her children or her husband were around her at all times. If a situation arose in which no one in her family was present, she would arrange to go out shopping or to visit a friend. Now that her last child was ready to move out and her husband was leaving more frequently on business trips, Molly was experiencing anxiety attacks at the thought of being alone. Being pregnant and the thought of having another child at home with her helped ease these feelings. Yet when she looked logically at her life, it did not make sense to have another child. Molly had heard of the spiritual abortion work and decided to find out more about it. She also hoped that this work would help her overcome her fear of being alone.

As Molly and I discussed her history, we could not find any conscious memory that seemed connected to her fear of being alone. Because of her religious upbringing, Molly did not believe in past lives, so we began the session with the intent of regressing to an unconscious childhood experience related to the fear. We also agreed to see in what other ways this pregnancy might be connected to her fear, and if the spirit had any information for her about this.

During the last phase of Spiritual Hypnosis trance induction, Molly found herself in a log cabin. When asked what she was wearing, she replied, "A kind of buckskin dress and bare feet." Although I suspected that this was a past life memory I did not say anything and proceeded to help Molly connect more deeply with this image. She said that she was about four years old and lived in the log cabin with her parents and grandmother. Her family was part of a small settlement with nothing but trees and new fields surrounding it. She witnessed an attack by a band of natives and watched her grandmother die from an arrow in her chest. In the chaos of the attack, Molly's parents directed her to hide in a type of root cellar until they came to get her. There, by herself, this little girl began to feel the same overwhelming terror that Molly experienced in her present-day form whenever she was alone.

To help Molly detach from the pain and fear of "being there," I instructed her to rise above the scene and watch it happening from above. Molly saw that the settlement was destroyed and her parents killed. She also saw that the terrified little girl remained in hiding until she died, still waiting for her parents to return. Molly realized that her little girl self had died with a deep fear of being left alone. I then took Molly back to that time so that she could "rerun" the scenario to change it. In this new scene everything happened as it had before, except when the attack was over, a kind angel-like woman came into the root cellar, took the little girl in her arms and comforted her. Then the woman gently took the little girl away to another life.

The session was powerful and Molly experienced a great deal of emotional release. She was now able to go into a place of deep peace and here meet with the spirit of the fetus. The message for her was that this pregnancy was meant to bring her to the place where she would have to deal with her fear of being alone. It was important for her to be free of this energy so that she could have the liberty to live life for herself. The spirit said that it did not wish to be born and had come for the purpose of helping her to become conscious. It told her that if she had just had an abortion without this work, her process would have been much more difficult.

After our session, Molly became concerned because she was uncomfortable with having what could be interpreted as a past-life experience. We talked about how her experience could instead be viewed as a metaphor or story symbolizing the trauma that the child within her experienced when left alone. This was easier for her to relate to. With past-life work, it is not the belief system, but the healing that occurs which is important. (The experiences that surface can be viewed as archetypal, past life, or genetic.) I use whatever lens the client is comfortable with.

In the weeks following our session, Molly experienced dramatic improvement. Molly had come to view the little girl in the session as symbolic of her own present-life inner child who needed to be mothered and made to feel safe. She did her "homework" which entailed spending time each day, nurturing, talking with, and creating a safe place for the abandoned little girl she had encountered in her session. Molly had done this for her own children, now it was time for her to do this for herself. As she did, her fears of being alone dissipated. Molly did proceed to have a clinical abortion and this went well for her. She felt at peace with her decision and healed quickly. Her big test came two weeks after the abortion when her husband was called out of town for a two-day meeting. In the past, Molly would have panicked and made frantic arrangements to fill her days. But now, though she did arrange a visit with a friend, she was able to focus on fun at-home activities that she could do by herself. She discovered that a part of her was even able to enjoy this time alone.

The Treasure

Anne first came to see me when she was about six weeks pregnant and quite unhappy. She had arranged to leave an unhealthy relationship only to discover she was pregnant. None of the alternatives she considered, including staying with her current partner and "making the best of it," becoming a single mother, or having an abortion, felt right to her. After reading about the Spiritual Approach to Abortion, she immediately contacted me and scheduled an appointment.

Anne and I began our first session with the usual methods of attaining deep awareness and relaxation. Anne soon found herself opening a large wooden door and stepping into a many-sided room. The large windows in each "facet" of the room allowed sunlight to stream inside. Piles of soft, brightly colored cushions scattered about the room gave it a friendly and inviting atmosphere. As Anne moved around noticing the colors, she became aware of a non-physical light presence which appeared to be feminine in nature. This Being was free-floating as it had not yet settled into physical existence. Anne was attracted to the softness of this presence and asked, "Are you the spirit child within me?" The affirmative answer was not actually spoken, but Anne felt it through her inner knowing. Anne explained why she was here and how she needed to leave the unhealthy relationship with her partner. She explained that having a child would serve no one involved at this time, but that she would gladly invite the spirit child in at another time when she was in the kind of relationship she wanted, with a man who would make a loving father. The spirit child seemed to understand and was happy to postpone physical incarnation. The spirit child then requested that Anne call forth her own inner child. Ann did this and looked on as a quiet, shy little girl stepped into the room. After some coaxing the little girl said that she was afraid that Anne, who had minimal contact with her now, would completely abandon her if she had a baby. The spirit child spoke saying, "You need to become acquainted with this little child, to nurture her and to play with her because when I return I do not want to take her place." Anne heard these words and then sat down with "Little" Anne on a pile of pillows. Anne and her inner child began to talk. Little Anne said that she wanted to wear pretty dresses and to go to the park and play on the swings. She also wanted to go for walks by the water, ride her bicycle, and have a soft cuddly teddy bear to hold. Adult Anne, with tears in her eyes, listened to and held her inner child. She told her that not only would she take care of her and do these things but that she would never leave her no matter how many babies she had. Little Anne, although happy, was also somewhat skeptical that this would happen. Anne felt her concern and asked how she could keep in contact with her. Little Anne said that she was always available as part of Anne's inner wisdom and that all Anne needed to do was to close her eyes and return to this room.

As Anne prepared to leave the room where she had spoken with her inner child, the spirit child reassured Anne that she had left the physical body. Anne then embraced her own inner child, aware that she had rediscovered a precious treasure. She had Little Anne "melt" into her heart where she would be safe, remembered, and surrounded with love.

As Anne opened the door to leave the room she discovered a long corridor. There was a sign with arrows pointing "this way to the uterus" and one pointing "this way to the brain." Anne chose to visit the uterus first. At the end of the hall she entered the uterus through a heavy, soft, thick, red velvet curtain. She found herself standing in a warm, dark room with red walls. As she lit a lantern she noticed a small man who then asked her why she was there. Anne explained to him her desire to release the pregnancy and that the spirit child had already receded from the fetus. The man agreed to help. She also wanted to see the fetus and asked the man if he would show it to her. He led her deeper into the room taking her to the place where the physical form of the spirit child rested. Anne described it as small, bean shaped and lifeless. Anne watched as the little man began to separate it from the uterine wall and she asked what else needed to be done. The little man showed her the mucous plug and said he could not remove it until he had help. Anne called upon her inner guide who came forth and indicated a willingness to help, but not until Anne was back home where she felt safe and supported. The little man agreed to wait and said that he would do all of the cleansing in preparation for the removal of the mucous plug. Anne thanked him for his help and with her guidance left the uterus to go visit the brain.

In the brain, Anne was greeted by a tall woman who informed her that she knew what had transpired between Anne and the spirit child and had already made appropriate adjustments. The woman advised Anne to check her breasts often throughout the miscarriage process, and to send love to her heart, drink as much water as she could, and get plenty of rest. Anne asked the woman if she could do something so that there wouldn't be any pain with this process. The woman assured Anne that she would assist in alleviating the pain.

Anne felt that she would miscarry at the time of her normal menstrual cycle and imagined the desired outcome with Future Pacing. (Future pacing is a technique where the hypnotherapist suggests that the client imagine a time in the future. The purpose is to see how the client responds to the session. In this case Anne imagined the time of her next menstrual cycle. When she did this she felt herself having the miscarriage.) She returned home and during the next week, which was the time of her normal menstrual period, she miscarried easily and with little discomfort.

Several years have passed and Anne is now married to a wonderful man whom she loves. Together they have a sweet little daughter. Is this the same soul that Anne met in the session? It well could be.

In Anne's session, I find it is interesting that a little man was the caretaker of the uterus and a tall woman the caretaker of the brain. In most sessions I have done it is exactly the opposite. One of the most powerful aspects of this work is that it does not follow any formula. It is always guided by spirit and that is what allows transformation to occur.

The Child in the Garden

Angie was pregnant for the third time in a six-month period. She had miscarried with her first pregnancy and had a clinical abortion with the second. She came to me for help in connecting with the spirit child so that she could learn from this experience.

After the session's trance induction, Angie stepped through a beautiful blue door into a lush garden full of tall, brightly colored flowers and softly singing birds. She started walking towards an ornately carved stone fountain at the garden's center. As she approached she could hear the sound of the water as it cascaded into the fountain's stone basin. Here a little girl was standing quietly by the fountain's edge. Angie knew this was the spirit child and started to cry as she knelt down beside her and told her how sorry she was that she did not want her in her life at this time. The spirit child told Angie, "I know all about you. I know you do not wish a child, but I wanted to come anyway to see what would happen." Angie asked why she had chosen her. The little girl answered, "Because you are so sweet and you have such a spiritual connection to life. I want a mother who is that way. I like you so much and want to stay with you."

Angie responded by telling the little girl how much she loved her, but that she could not be her mother and did not wish to have a child at this time. Angie then asked if this being had come to her before and learned that she had been present before at one other time. Angie told the spirit child that she deserved to find a mother who was willing to bring her forth into the physical world. The little girl sadly acknowledged that this was true and that she would have to go from this place. She also let Angie know how much she was enjoying this contact with her. Angie took a moment to hold her in her arms. She felt that this Being was a part of her in a very special way and that they were both a gift to each other. While held in Angie's arms, the spirit child said that she was afraid that Angie would focus upon the loss rather than remember the loving communication they had shared. Angie thanked the little girl and said that she would do her best to focus on what was gained from this rather than what was lost. The spirit child then receded and the garden became quiet and still.

Angie left the garden and proceeded along a pathway to the uterus. She stepped through a pink triangular door into a cylindrically shaped cave with soft pink walls. She looked up and noticed the caretaker was a non-physical energy floating near the top of the cave. Angie addressed her as "Womb Mother." This being was aware of all that had happened. She informed Angie that she had already begun to cleanse the uterine lining from the walls. Angie thanked her for her care and support and asked if Womb Mother would now be willing to help with releasing all the tissue. Womb Mother floated down from the top of the cave and slowly took human form. Angie could feel Womb Mother's compassion for her and they embraced. Womb Mother said that she would need assistance with the overall process and wanted Angie to be a part of it. "Angie," she said, "it is important for you to remember that your body is an important part of yourself and that it really does desire to work with you. Your body is your friend."

Angie asked about the mucous plug and Womb Mother replied that she would need Angie's help to release it. They both stepped over and leaned against it. Angie enjoyed working with her body in this way and started to feel the energy move. Angie asked how she could stay open to communication with Womb Mother. "My dear one," replied Womb Mother, "just bring to your mind an image of the two of us embracing."

After visiting the uterus, Angie stepped out of the cave and found herself on another path where she encountered a plain white door with the words "HORMONE CONTROL" written on the outside. She pushed open the door and entered a dimly lit, lavender colored padded room. A scientist in a white lab coat was in charge here and so engrossed in her work that she did not notice her visitor until Angie tapped her lightly on the shoulder. The scientist turned, smiled, and extended a hand to greet her. Angie commented upon the efficient job that she was doing. The scientist replied that she liked her job very much and enjoyed making things run smoothly. After she was informed about the meetings with both the spirit child and Womb Mother, the scientist knew that the work she had been doing to prepare the body for this pregnancy was no longer necessary. Angie asked if the scientist would be willing to reverse the process and return her body back to its non-pregnant state. "Yes, I accept your situation and do not foresee any problem," the scientist replied. "I could not have helped you if you had not told me of your situation and asked for assistance. Now that I have this information I am able to change it over at the control center. What I will do will help your body return to it's regular and normal cycles." They both entered a room where there were multicolored dials and switches. The scientist adjusted the progesterone and estrogen levers and informed Angie that she would check hourly to make certain the hormones were at the proper pre-pregnancy levels. The scientist then asked Angie if she had spoken with her hypothalamus gland. Angie replied that she had not, so the scientist pointed the way to another door with the sign "HYPOTHALAMUS" on it.

Angie knocked on the hypothalamus door and then entered. It was a dimly lit and oddly shaped room with five sides and a very low ceiling. She walked to the front of the room where the light was better and noticed a short person sitting in a chair. This person was an energetic and ageless being, possessing qualities of both youth and old age. The person motioned for Angie to have a seat. This guide greeted Angie and then said, "It is good that you have come to see me to check your overall state of health." Angie liked and trusted this being. The guide explained to her that a fluid was excreted here and served as a chemical communication throughout the body. The guide further explained how, because of inner stress, the impulses had not been steady enough and the overall health of the body had become weak. This had left Angie feeling out of sync with herself and her surrounding environment. "Regulation of these impulses gives a feeling of oneness within and without," the guide told Angie. The guide also told Angie that her help was needed for the hypothalamus to work properly. "I want you to feel your whole body working together. It's like the feeling you have when you are in meditation posture. Your serenity and sense of oneness will help me to regulate this." Angie then spent several minutes in silence learning from her guide. When she again spoke, she told me that she felt a very clear communication with this part of herself and that she could easily contact this guide during meditation so that they could work together.

Both Angie and I felt very positive after her session. We both believed that there would be no difficulty in releasing the unneeded tissue. However, three days later she called to tell me that she was still having morning sickness. The condition continued for another three days so we decided to meet for a second session.

Once more Angie entered into that deep state of relaxation where she met with the hormone control scientist. This time the scientist was waiting for Angie. "You have been doing a good job of being in touch with your body, however the symptoms of pregnancy remain because you are stuck back in the moment when you met the spirit child in the garden. Every time I shift the hormone levels, you cause them to shift back to pregnancy levels. You are stopping this process because you want to feel what it is to be a child again." Angie acknowledged that when she met the little girl she had felt a great warmth in her heart and wanted to be like her. The scientist gently said, "What you need to do is to go and meet your inner child. She is that part of you who is innocent and sweet and is always with you and available to you. You need not be pregnant to be with her and feel her love. She is here waiting to meet you, may I invite her in now?"

Angie felt a little nervous, but was willing to meet her inner child. The door opened and Little Angie appeared dressed in jeans with a white T-shirt with sandals on her feet and pink ribbons in her hair. Angie quickly walked over and picked her up. "She is the essence of me and I feel sad because I don't know how to be more like her. She is the part of me that likes to play and that feels light and happy, never worried or concerned. How can I have you more in my life? I love you very much! " Little Angie replied, " It is not a problem for me to be part of your life. You are human and I am part of being human. I want you to play with me and hold me."

Angie continued to speak with her inner child and together they went to an inner playground where they could run, swing, slide and just be with each other in the sunshine. Angie was taking the first steps in reclaiming her playful, sweet, and innocent nature from this little girl. Little Angie reminded her of childhood feelings long forgotten. I had Angie imagine having this child with her in her present day life at work, at home alone and with her partner. When it was time to end the session Angie brought this inner child fully into her being by allowing her to melt into her heart center. She promised to spend time with this little one every day, to listen to and make her an active part of her life. While Angie was bonding with her inner child, I sensed the presence of the spirit child and her delight that Angie had returned to be with her own inner child. This spirit child had given Angie a wonderful gift.

The scientist was pleased with this communication. However, Angie confided to her that, although she felt a strong connection with her inner child, she was still feeling some doubt about this process working. The scientist understood and told Angie that this was a process of learning about herself and her needs, and that at this very moment, while they were speaking her body was adjusting back to normal. Angie asked if there was a sign that her body could give to boost her confidence in the success of the process. At this moment Angie experienced a tingling sensation in her legs and a warmth in her lower back. The scientist confirmed that these were signs that the body was indeed returning to its natural non-pregnant state. She recommended that Angie play with her inner child over the next few days to deepen the bond and experience reality. She was told that this would help her body complete the process. We finished the session by future-pacing (a technique where the client visualizes a future event) both this bonding and the miscarriage process. Everything checked as complete at this time.

Angie reported several days later that she noticed a new lightness in her life and realized that this child part of her allowed her to give and receive love more easily. She also informed me that she had made the choice to have a clinical abortion. Her body had not yet started to release the tissue on it's own. Even though she felt that the spirit child wishing to incarnate was no longer present, she decided that it was time to take this more traditional route. After the abortion, she told me that because of the traumatic experience of her first abortion she had been terrified that, someday, she would have to face that again. However, she said that because of her work with the Spiritual Abortion process this abortion was an entirely different experience. Instead of feeling overwhelmed by fear and guilt, she moved through this second abortion feeling more empowered, peaceful, and certain of her choice.

In many cases this work leads to a natural abortion and a clinical abortion is not needed. However, it appears that in some cases a clinical abortion is necessary for personal growth.

Soul Contracts

Section VI

In Conclusion

Sun and Moon
       and your own heart
speak always of that which abides.
       In solitude and stillness
       Know that the journey
begins and ends
       with the self

                    Ralph Blum

Is It Real?

"The things we see," Pistorius said softly, "are the same things that are within us. There is no reality except the one contained within us. That is why so many people live such unreal lives. They take the images outside them for reality and never allow the world within to assert itself." Herman Hesse, Demian

Now that you have read these stories and my theories concerning them, the skeptic in you might ask, "Is any of this real?" To answer that question we need to define the term "real."

In the *New Merriam-Webster Dictionary*, third edition, "real" is defined as:

1: fact, actually being or existent
2: not artificial: genuine.

In *Webster's New 20th Century Unabridged Dictionary*, "real" is defined as:

1: Actually being or existing, not fictitious or imaginary; as a description of *real* life.
2: True, genuine; not counterfeit, or fictitious. In such pursuits lie *real* honor and the nation's glory. -Robert Fulton. *Real* presence: in various churches the actual presence of the body and blood of Christ in the Eucharist, or the conversion of the substance of the bread and wine into the real body and blood of Christ.

Even the dictionary contains definitions of *real* that one may or may not agree with. Who is to define what *real* life might be, or what *real* honor or presence are? Most of us can agree on our experience of physical reality, such as the realness of a chair we are sitting on or the table holding our dinner, but outside of the obvious, physical realm we have disagreement.

A friend of mine lost her mother several years ago. She had gone for her usual weekly visit and found her mother lying dead upon the floor. The memory of this experience caused her great discomfort, sadness, and even depression until her mother "visited" her several weeks later and told her to stop worrying. Her mother said that she was very happy where she was and would be there to greet my friend when it was her time to come. Was this a real visitation, or only a figment of my friend's imagination? I cannot say. But, what I do know is that my friend had never before had such an experience and that after this experience she was her "old self," the deep sadness and uncomfortable memories were gone.

When I address the topic of past lives in my classes, students always want to know if they are really real. I always reply that I do not know. I can talk about my experiences and beliefs, but they are mine and come through my filter. As a group we then discuss our experiences, beliefs, and the alternative possibilities.

You may have heard the term "the collective unconscious." This term refers to the idea that we are all connected with each other and with every living thing on the planet. Once, at a lecture, I heard Depak Chopra say that as we breathe we breathe out cells of our liver, lungs, heart and other organs and we likewise breathe in those cells from others around us. Because we have always done this, says Chopra, all of us contain a number of cells from Jesus, from Buddha, and from countless others throughout time. Through our collective unconscious we can connect with everyone who lives and has lived before us. We can enter a quiet place within where knowledge from throughout the ages is available to us. From this point of view, when one experiences a past life, the memory is not coming from a personal past life, but rather from the greater consciousness accessed via cellular memory. Thus, the experiences held in our bodies are not necessarily "ours" in a personal sense.

The collective unconscious explains the "I was a famous person in my past life" experience. Numerous people have proclaimed that they were Saint Joan of Arc, Cleopatra, Napoleon, Mary Magdaline, Michaelangelo, or some other well known personality. I have known several people who have claimed to have been the same historical figure. How could this be? It may be that their present lives feel a bit mundane, they want to impress others, or bolster their own ego; sometimes when this is the case, these people give themselves permission to deny their creative potential in this life because of who they were in the past. Of course, it could be also that there is truth in what those people claim. A great part of their spirits may be connected to one of these well known personalities, and therefore they can more easily draw upon memories or resources from these persons than can those who are not as connected. Major personalities seem to have very powerful spirits and perhaps that is why many people can experience "being" such personalities.

In addition to the collective unconscious and past life theories, there is the theory that time is not linear and that past, present, and future are all happening at once. I find this theory fascinating and as plausible as any but my mind hasn't been able to grasp it. If you are interested in exploring this further, I recommend Richard Bach's book *One*. This book provides an enjoyable, well crafted portrayal of the subject.

Then there is the heaven and hell perspective, and other theories that do not support the notion of past-lives. With these belief systems, all we have is this one time to be in the physical body and then we die. What happens next? It depends on which school of thought you come from. For some it is nothing, there is no soul and the body returns to dust and that's the end of the show. For others, it means that the soul is freed and, depending upon how good or bad you were, you go happily to be with God or to suffer eternally in hell.

I do not pretend to know what "the reality" is. Maybe what we believe helps to determine what our reality is. So, are past lives real? Only you can answer that for yourself based upon your own experiences. I am not here to try and prove or disprove anyone else's beliefs or theories. I can only state what is true for me. My belief is that our spirit does continue lifetime after lifetime. I believe that there are a number of possibilities to this. We may contain pieces of, or have connections with, many spirits. I also believe that we incarnate with people, or souls, that we have had relationships with in the past and that these souls assist us in our development as we assist them in theirs. From my personal experiences, this appears to be an accurate view, and it has been my belief and is the belief this book is based upon.

Sometimes a belief can be held so strongly that it is accepted as the truth without ever being challenged. Many years ago, for example, I held the belief that it was impossible to walk over a bed of red-hot coals without getting seriously burnt. This appeared to be a solid truth, until the first time I walked across a fire without getting burnt. This shattered my previous reality. I experienced a huge release of emotion and something in my brain actually shifted. I then wondered, "What other limiting beliefs do I accept as absolute truth?" Now I lead firewalks so that others may experience the teaching of the fire and move through their limitations and fears.

Throughout the pages of this book we see that the circumstances of our lives are not about a God who punishes or rewards us for the actions that *we* judge to be good or bad. Instead, every choice we make holds an opportunity for our soul's personal growth. Maybe hell is only a pattern of guilt, judgement and suffering that is repeated lifetime after lifetime and heaven is the freedom from this pattern.

God, the Great Spirit, is a loving energy that supports our growth, our desires to heal, to love and to live in accordance with our true nature. Through this work in Spiritual Hypnosis I have watched myself, my students and my clients release old, unwanted patterns, grow in consciousness and self-love and live in greater spiritual harmony with God, Goddess and all that is.

*From miracles you were made
and to mystery you shall return.*

an Ancient Mystic

Some Definitions

These are my personal definitions for words as used in this book. They are my definitions, and I dispute no one who defines these words differently.

Great Spirit, God/Goddess, God Source, Universal Intelligence, Universal Energy

That which is part of everything and that which we are a part of. That which knows the "big picture." That whose plan we are a part of.

Spirit/spirit

When capitalized I am speaking of the Great Spirit. In lower case, spirit may refer to the human soul or to any essence that is of the non-physical realm.

spirit guides

Those energies whose purpose is to guide us. These guides are personal and appear as angels, animals, elders, or whichever form best serves the one receiving guidance.

soul

The spirit part of ourselves. That part which is made in the image and likeness of God. The soul is the part of ourselves that slips into a physical body each time we incarnate. The soul is our higher self and connects our physical being with the God Source.

higher self

Our soul self and our connection to the infinite wisdom of the God Source.

Appendix

For those of you interested in pursuing this work more deeply, or if you have questions, or comments, you may write to:

Linda Baker
1202 N. 35th Street,
Renton, Washington 98056-1964.
or e-mail to: lindabak@hotmail.com

You may purchase the audio tape:

Abortion-A Spiritual Approach

© 1991 (Side A: Abortion-A Spiritual Appro-ach and Side B: Healing from Past Miscarriage/Abortion) by Linda Baker, by mailing a check for $12.00 to the above address.

If you are interested in pursuing comprehensive, spiritually based hypnotherapy as a career, or to add these skills to your current practice, please contact:

The Hypnotherapy Institute
2732 N. Nelson,
Spokane, Washington 99207

You may E-mail the school at: HypnoInst@aol.com

or access our website at: hypnotherapyinstitute.org

The Hypnotherapy Institutes
of Spokane and Seattle

The Hypnotherapy Institutes of Spokane and Seattle provide students with comprehensive training in hypnotherapy. This training includes clinical approaches to hypnotherapy as well as the Spiritual Hypnotherapy tools used in the sessions described in this book.

The Institutes' basic, 200 hour training includes the following classes:

1. Introduction to Hypnotherapy & basic Hypnosis Skills
2. Solution Focused Counseling
3. Etheric Plane Communication, Emotional Clearing & Working with Resistance
4. In-Depth Inner Child
5. Healing the Inner Child/Regression Techniques
6. Inner Guides, Inner Mate & Inner Harmony (balance of the feminine & masculine energies)
7. Past-Life Regression
8. Sub-Personality Therapy
9. Addictions
10. Light Mind/Light Body Weight Release
11. Establishing a Practice and Counseling Assessments

In addition to this basic training, the Institutes offer a wide variety of advanced classes. All classes are presented at the licensed vocational schools in Seattle and Spokane. Certification is provided through the American Council of Hypnotist Examiners, the National Board of Hypnotherapy, and The National Board for Hypnotherapy and Hypnotic Anaesthesiology.

Classes are offered in both weekend and evening formats. A correspondence course may also be added. This course would require a residential intensive seg-ment in either Seattle or Spokane. If you are interested in this course, or in sponsoring one or more of our classes in your area, please contact the school at the above physical or electronic address.

Judy Ward is the owner and director of the Hypnotherapy Institutes of Spokane and Seattle, as well as an instructor. Deborah Kaye and Linda Baker are instructors for the school. All three women continue to offer private sessions for clients in both the Seattle and Spokane areas.

I encourage anyone who has an interest in writing, whether it be personal or for publication to call

Write From the Heart Seminars
with
Hal Zina Bennett and Susan J. Sparrow
1-800-738-6721

Ask to receive their publication
Opening Inward

Hal and Susan are dedicated to personal empowerment through expression and self knowledge. Their writing seminars are powerful, creative experiences that truly allow their students to write from the heart.

About the Author

Linda and her husband Tom, live in a rustic, hunting lodge which was built in 1925 and overlooks Lake Washington and the Olympic Mountain Range. Here they enjoy their gardens and making their space available to the many people who come to their center for a wide variety of classes and healing sessions.

Linda and Tom are the parents of two grown children and have foster parented many teenaged children over a period of nineteen years.

Linda, among other things, loves nature, gardening, writing, art work and walking several miles each day. Besides her professional work she networks and gives time in service to others.